Music in Worship

Music
in
Worship

A Mennonite Perspective

Edited by Bernie Neufeld

Herald Press

Herald Press
Scottdale, Pennsylvania
Waterloo, Ontario

Faith & Life Press
Newton, Kansas
Winnipeg, Manitoba

Library of Congress Cataloging-in-Publication Data

Neufeld, Bernie
Music in Worship, edited by Bernie Neufeld.
p. cm.
ISBN 0-8361-9459-4 (alk. paper)

BX8128.C49C66 1998
289.7'3—de21   97-12503

The paper used in this publication is recycled and meets the minimum requirements of American National Standard for Information Sciences—Permanence of Paper for Printed Library Materials, ANSI Z39.48-1984.

Scripture quotations are from the *New Revised Standard Version Bible*, copyright © 1989 by the Division of Christian Education of the National Council of Churches of Christ in the USA and are used by permission.

MUSIC IN WORSHIP
Copyright © 1998 by Herald Press, Scottdale, Pa. 15683
All rights reserved
Printed in the United States of America
Library of Congress Catalog Number: 97-12503
International Standard Book Number: 0-8361-9459-4
Cover design by Gwen Stamm
Book design by Jim Butti

1 2 3 4 5 6 7 8 9 10 01 00 99 98

To Marg, Byron, LeAnn and Kevin,
who graciously supported me in my
ministry through music in the church.

Contents

Preface

Jesus: *But the hour is coming, and is now here, when the true worshipers will worship the Father in spirit and truth, for the Father seeks such as these to worship him. God is spirit, and those who worship him must worship in spirit and in truth. (John 4:23-24)*

Paul: *May the God of steadfastness and encouragement grant you to live in harmony with one another, in accordance with Christ Jesus, so that together you may with one voice glorify the God and Father of our Lord Jesus Christ. (Rom. 15:5-6)*

Jesus, a Jew, responds to a controversial question asked by a Samaritan woman about where people should worship if it were to be done properly. In the Gospel of John (4:20), she states: "Our ancestors worshiped on this mountain, but you say that . . ." Jesus' response was not likely what she wanted to hear. Jesus' reply took the discussion in the direction of the **what** and the **why** rather than the **how** or the **where**. Jesus put his finger on a very sensitive spot, for neither locale nor cultural concerns are important— God looks for people who "worship the Father in spirit and truth." In our churches today, we have been caught up with concerns similar to those of the woman at the well, and that is probably due to the fact that we have in our congregations people of diverse cultural backgrounds or those who simply have very different views of worship. Simple solutions are not easily found.

The apostle challenges followers of Jesus Christ to live in peace and harmony with one another. Romans 14 and 15 lay down some crucial principles: "Welcome those who are weak in the faith, but not for the purpose of quarreling over opinions" (Rom. 14:1). All of us will stand or fall before our Lord, who is able to make us stand (v. 4). People are to be allowed freely to make up their own minds (v. 5). We are not to live only for ourselves (v. 7). We are not to judge one another, for we will all be judged by God (vv. 10-13). Avoid being a stumbling block to others (vv. 13-15, 21). The kingdom of God consists of righteousness, peace, and joy in the Holy Spirit, not food and drink (v. 17). Our goal should be to pursue peace and to build each other up (v. 19, Rom. 15:1-3). We are to welcome each other as Christ has welcomed us (v. 7).

At a time in our history where the most important thing is to "look after number one," or at best to tolerate another's point of view, the call to defend the special interests of another person seem rather unrealistic. How does the church deal with diversity of thought and practice concerning the place of music in worship? How can we discover and reinstitute the biblical call to defend the interests of another person rather than our own? Romans 15:7 points us in a specific direction—we are to do all of the above "for the glory of God." Marva J. Dawn in *Reaching Out Without Dumbing Down* discusses worship in our present culture, passionately pointing out that what we need most is to get back to worshiping God (Wm. B. Eerdmans Pub. Co., 1995, p. 76-82).

The main purpose of this book is to be a resource for pastors, worship leaders, and church musicians in local congregations (song leaders, praise and worship teams, choir directors, music/worship committees, soloists, ensembles, instrumentalists). The second purpose is to provide a resource for church music courses taught at colleges, universities, and seminaries.

Some of the chapters address the theological and philosophical nature of music's place in worship; others are more practical in nature. The vision from the very beginning has been to develop an understanding of the role of music in the church today and to speak from an Anabaptist and Mennonite perspective. At the same time, we hope that worshiping communities of other faith traditions will benefit from this resource.

I am deeply indebted to the following persons and organizations: Canadian Mennonite Bible College Board and faculty; my consultation group consisting of Robert J. Suderman, Doreen Klassen, George D. Wiebe, and Rudy Schellenberg; the Congregational Resources Board of the Conference of Mennonites in Canada; Adolf Ens and Margaret Franz for their constant words of encouragement and advice; Karen Guenther for doing the major editing of this book; all the writers who were asked to submit a chapter as "a gift to the church"; and last but certainly not least, my wife, Margaret, for her patience, encouragement, and critique, as well as the countless hours she spent typing and retyping chapters or portions thereof. *–Bernie Neufeld*

Chapter 1

Worship:
True to Jesus

by Eleanor Kreider

Most Christians claim that their worship is rooted in the Bible. We deeply desire to be true to biblical values in prayer and praise. We ferret out texts and patterns. In varied ways Christians have searched for the simplicity, truth, mystery, and power we sense as we read of worship in the New Testament.

The sisters of Grandchamp Community, in the Reformed tradition, seek to express in their monastic life of prayer, the spirit, the content, and the forms of New Testament prayer. In their Rule, they call themselves "to pray and work for the kingdom," "to maintain the interior silence of abiding in Christ," and "to penetrate the spirit of the Beatitudes—joy, simplicity, mercy."

Anabaptist groups in the sixteenth century looked to Acts 2:42 for a worship model. "They devoted themselves to the apostles' teaching and fellowship, to the breaking of bread and the prayers." What a simple form, doing only what is necessary for truly Christian worship! They also washed one another's feet and sang hymns, both of which have precedents in Scripture. The New Testament gave them authority for free, participative worship offered to God in sincerity and truth.

Spare and simple forms, however, are not the only consequence of a search for biblical authenticity in worship. Eastern Orthodox worship also displays close attention to biblical precedents. It perpetuates essential elements and basic structures of worship practices of the earliest apostolic church. The two main movements in their worship, called entrances, focus on Scripture and thanksgiving. Cantors and congregation sing Bible passages and ministers preach the application to people's everyday lives. Their great thanksgiving prayer at the eucharist, highly developed through long tradition, focuses on the overarching biblical story of redemption. Christ's presence is honored in the Gospel readings; he is represented in the person of the priest; he is mystically present in the eucharist; he is visually presented overhead, enthroned in glory. Orthodox Christians join their worship with that of the saints and angels in heaven. The whole cosmos reverberates in the magnificent blend of light, color, incense, music, and movement. For Eastern Christians this is biblical worship, powerfully evoked in the book of Revelation.

Christians say that we root our worship in the New Testament. But are we as true to the New Testament as we think? Maybe we are. But let's consider this question.

Are we as true to the New Testament as we think?

The New Testament is not a book of common prayer. It is a compendium of writings with a variety of purposes. It is not a ministers' handbook for ordering worship services. But the Bible is a book marvelously rich in materials about worship and for worship.

The Old Testament preserves and describes many ways in which the Hebrews worshiped God. The Psalms, the Books of the Law, and the prophetic writings record teaching about worship. They prescribe festivals. They preserve prayers and songs of individuals and communities of God's people across many centuries.

The New Testament, too, is a mine of worship in the

widest sense. That means that we understand worship to involve not only the words, songs, and feelings of the worshiping community itself. True biblical worship is a living demonstration of how praise and honor to God is lived out within the body of Christ. True biblical worship flows outward in prophetic truth and self-giving love to the world around it. This is the full witness of God's worshiping people.

If the New Testament, then, is not a prayer book or a book of common order, in what ways can it properly act as a source for worship today? How can we make appropriate connections? While not expecting to find prescriptions, we can learn about the ethos and inner meanings of early Christian worship.

Prophetic and ecstatic worship in Revelation

In Revelation, the book of the Apocalypse, the new Christian community creates a vigorous interpretation of its own times. It makes this critique within worship. It is hard for us to imagine the first political impact of the assertion: God alone is worthy of worship! The book of Revelation has many liturgical dimensions. To worship is to sing and to confess, in God's presence, that there is salvation in bleak times. It is to acclaim God as Ruler over all things. It is to break the enchantment of the world and its power. To sing the songs of Revelation is to interpret the meaning of contemporary events, to critique the times. All of this adds up to worship in its broadest biblical sense. This is worship that connects God, the Holy One, with humans and all of God's natural creation.

Testimonies, stories, and advice

We know that in worship in the earliest communities, Christians gave testimonies, preserved memories, and passed on the Gospel stories. How else would we know about Stephen's stoning, about the women at the foot of the cross, or about Paul's undignified escape over the Damascus city wall? In worship they repeated the preciously harbored materials which we now call the Gospels. They read out wise advice and encouragement that came to them in the form of pastoral letters. Testimonies, stories, letters, advice, and encouragement—all these were integrated into New Testament worship.

In their worship patterns, varied communities reflected differences in culture, customs, and language. Unlike others, the community of the Gospel of John preserved the upper room memory with the ceremony of foot washing. Patterns of worship leadership were not fixed. Prayers and blessings sprang out of intense experiences of persecution, growth, struggle, and joy. And so we find immensely varied and colorful fragments of worship, reflecting new communities of differing languages, cultures, and customs.

We do not find structures and patterns, templates, grids, or rubrics. Rather, we find single words, fragments, and bits of creeds, hymns, prayers, and references to rites such as baptism, communion, and foot washing. It is all so tantalizing. How we would love to know more details!

The fragments we do find are rich and revealing about the inner meanings and the fervent ethos in worship. The meanings are pastorally communal and pointedly political. Here are a few examples:

Pastoral and political meanings in worship

The most beloved New Testament hymn is the basis for numerous later songs and church hymns: "Christ Jesus, who, though he was in the form of God, did not regard equality with God as something to be exploited, but emptied himself" (Phil. 2:5-7). Equally exalted in praise of Christ are these outbursts of praise: "He is the image of the invisible God, the firstborn of all creation" (Col. 1:15f.); "Sleeper, awake! Rise from the dead, and Christ will shine on you" (Eph. 5:14);

"He was put to death in the flesh, but made alive in the

spirit" (1 Pet.3:18).

Singing these hymns, early Christians reminded themselves of the matchless character of their Lord and of the quality of their life together, as they formed the body of Christ. Imagine early Christians chanting the Beatitudes, repeating the great commandment together, and aligning their common life to the teaching and model of their Lord Jesus. To abide in his love; that was their goal. They surely sang of his love and aspired to his way of love in their hymns. Worship built up the common life.

The shortest biblical creed makes a sharp political point: "Jesus is Lord." (not Caesar!) (Rom. 10:9). Unlike the kingdoms of this world, "the kingdom of God is . . . righteousness and peace and joy in the Holy Spirit" (Rom. 14:17). Another creed packs the mystery of our faith into six short phrases: "He was revealed in flesh, vindicated in spirit, seen by angels, proclaimed among Gentiles, believed in throughout the world, taken up in glory" (1 Tim. 3:16). What a vast vision! In worship Christians could receive and keep things in proper perspective. God's reign extends over the whole of human life and natural creation.

Given these examples, how would we define a hymn? A hymn was in no sense a fixed composition. A New Testament hymn or fragment of hymn is just one tiny part of what must have been a great swelling up of prayer and praise expressed in poetic speech. C. F. D. Moule gives a wonderful image: It is impossible to experience a horse galloping from looking at one still frame. So it is with New Testament hymnody. We never see a running of the film, but just selected still frames. What we do see, snapshots of praise that arose within the spontaneity of worship, fuse together within the New Testament text.

Blessings, rites, and patterns of readings

Numerous prayers and blessings are scattered throughout the letters of the New Testament. Besides the most familiar benedictions, a few further samples are: "I pray

that . . . God . . . may give you a spirit of wisdom and revelation as you come to know him" (Eph. 1:17ff.); "Blessed
be the God . . . who has blessed us in Christ with every spiritual blessing" (Eph. 1:3); "Blessed be the . . . Father of mer-
cies and the God of all consolation" (2 Cor. 1:3f.).

We have references to baptism, six times in the book of
Acts, though no descriptions of the rite. The accounts of
Jesus' mandate for eucharistic celebration appear in four
places: "Do this to remember me." The Gospel of John
records Jesus' disconcerting action of washing his disciples' feet and his instructions that they were to do the same
to one another. Unlike other rites, this one is described in
some detail.

Some scholars have suggested that certain parts of the
New Testament represent patterns of readings used in worship. One lectionary theory argues that the Gospel of John
or the Gospel of Matthew were systematic readings based
perhaps on synagogue patterns or that they were festal
readings around the Jewish-Christian year. Was the passion
story told and read in its entirety at eucharistic worship?
Perhaps 1 Peter was a baptismal homily. These are tantalizing suggestions.

Jesus is the measure of our worship

In summary then, the New Testament is a lively product of worshiping communities. Its literary footprints do
not reveal specific patterns for worship but do give important clues about the content, ethos, and values of the praise
and prayer of the first Christian communities.

The primary theme of New Testament worship, the
thread that runs through all, is devotion to Jesus Christ,
who was acknowledged as Messiah and Lord. Worship
texts and rites always point to this one person. Who was
Jesus? How could new Christians express their relationship to him? If the central meaning of New Testament worship texts, its binding quality, is Jesus, then to be true to the
New Testament in our worship, we too must look to Jesus

as the measure of our worship.

We will consider three claims about Jesus that the New Testament communities passionately asserted in letters, testimonies, and stories. These texts help us to understand their everyday life and faith and also their worship. As we do this, we can consider these three claims as measures for our own contemporary worship.

Jesus is Messiah

Jesus is Messiah. This was a dramatic claim. A number of songs and stories in the Gospels reveal what such a claim meant to people. How they longed for and prayed for the liberation that Messiah would bring!

Zechariah's prophetic words over the infant John (Luke 1:68-79) give us a sense of this intense hope for Messiah. "You, child, . . . will go before the Lord to prepare his ways, to give knowledge of salvation to his people by the forgiveness of their sins" (vv. 76-77). And our hearts leap with Simeon's as he recognizes the identity of the infant Jesus: "my eyes have seen your salvation" (Luke 2:30).

The disciples Martha and Peter each exclaimed, "You are . . . Messiah!" (Matt. 16:16; John 11:27). Jesus himself confessed his royal identity to the high priest at the trial (Mark 14:62). What a range of expectation, joy, doubt, and hope centered on this figure—the one sent from God to set his people free.

In the Emmaus-road conversation, Jesus spelled it out as clearly as possible. The dejected disciples blurted out, "Jesus was a prophet mighty in deed and word before God and all the people . . . We had hoped that he was the one to redeem Israel." Then Jesus himself explained from Moses and the prophets everything about himself, how it was necessary (in the divine purpose) that the Messiah should suffer and then enter into his glory (Luke 24: 13-29).

The meaning of Messiah's role became clearer after the resurrection and Pentecost. The Christians realized that Jesus had interpreted his messianic role according to the

Servant Songs of Isaiah (e.g. Isa. 42; 49; 50; 52-53). He was Messiah, not only for Israel, but also for many (peoples), for all (peoples). We hear it in the words of institution, "This is my blood of the covenant, which is poured out for many for the forgiveness of sins" (Matt. 26:28). We see Jesus' messianic passion for justice and true worship in the temple-cleansing incident. God's house was to be a "house of prayer for all nations." Jesus' calling was the focus of Israel's calling—to be the light toward which all nations would turn. Messiah Jesus' deepest commitment was to fulfill his calling to reconcile the world to God.

What did it mean for the first Christians to say, "Jesus is Messiah"? It meant to remember and repeat the stories of Jesus (e.g., temple cleansing and walk to Emmaus). It meant to interpret events of history (e.g., Simeon, Zechariah). It meant to put things into the big context (e.g., Peter, Martha). We can see the vision of the New Testament believers gradually opening up. Peter in Acts 10 welcomes the Roman centurion. An enemy becomes a brother. Paul's passionate vision, too, was for the integration of Gentiles into the body of Christ. Forgiveness and reconciliation was for "many" and for "all," just as Jesus had said.

We tell the whole story in worship

To draw on this big vision is to tell the story, the whole story of God with Israel, the story of the Creation, the Fall, and redemption. It means to grasp what the disciples did on the Emmaus road and to interpret where Jesus belongs in the great story of God's redemptive love. It means to continue the story on into our own historical period.

We might think of the shape of a great Shakespearean drama. We Christians are involved in a vast drama with five acts. We already know the first four acts: the Creation, the Fall, Israel, Jesus. Now Act 5 is on stage. It has begun with Pentecost. Our job is to write and act out one of the scenes of Act 5. We must do it in the context of the whole drama. Our scene must be consistent with the main plot that we already know. The action in our scene must be relevant to the character of the entire story.

To say "Jesus is Messiah" required the early Christians, and it requires us as their inheritors, to tell the whole wonderful story, to interpret its implications—salvation, redemption, and forgiveness—and to incarnate the story. That means we have to carry on the story of Messiah, every day of our lives.

I suggest we hold on to the name Messiah. I have heard some people object, "Messiah? That's a Jewish word. It's not English. It's archaic. Jesus was the Jew's Messiah; he did what he had to do. Finished. Calling Jesus 'Messiah' probably satisfied the Jewish Christians and made sense to them. But it really has nothing to do with us. Delete 'Messiah' and call him 'Christ.' Let that just be a part of the name of Jesus, his last name—Jesus Christ."

But I think we should use the name Messiah and tell Messiah's story. We should tell the story of Israel's longing, exile, and hopelessness. We should tell the story of the Spirit's reappearance and of Jesus. Let's interpret the story of the Messiah Jesus, and carry it on in our communities. Let's use the mission statement of Messiah Jesus in Luke 4:18-19. Memorize it. Sing it. Pray it.

Communion service tells the story

Preeminently we tell, interpret, and carry on the Messiah's story in the communion service. This gift of Jesus to the church enables us to know who we are, to know God's love and forgiveness, to fulfill our sense of belonging in unity to one another, to rejoice in Jesus' presence in the Spirit, and to prepare to express God's reconciling love to the "many" and the "all"—the whole world whom God loves. In communion we enact the whole trajectory of God's story—from Creation to Passover meal, through the events of Jesus' Last Supper and the early Christian fellowship meals, onward to the great messianic banquet of the kingdom when people will come from the East and West, North and South to feast at the Lord's table. Our communion services are appetizers for that great banquet.

Jesus is Lord

Jesus is Lord. This confession may have been most characteristic of Gentile Christians. We find it recorded twice (Rom. 10:9; 1 Cor. 12:3). Opinions differ. Was this a liturgical acclamation? Was it a statement used in courts in which Christians had to bear witness? Was it part of a baptismal liturgy? Was it used in worship assembly? We don't know.

But we're pretty sure what it was not. It was not a vote in an election: "Please designate the rabbi of your choice." It was not just a part of Jesus' name: "Lord Jesus." To us it might sound like a title of nobility: Sir Jesus or Lord Jesus of Nazareth. No! This was neither a matter of choosing a local official nor merely a term of honor.

It was much more! In whatever context this phrase was used, it was a statement of allegiance. We know the rival confession: "Caesar is Lord." Sometimes Christians, if asked to declare "Caesar is Lord," were compelled to "curse Christ," to anathematize Jesus. If Christians replied "Jesus is Lord," they made a political challenge. It was cheeky, provocative, and dangerous.

In some places Christians could honestly say, "We are good citizens. We pay our taxes. Our lives are above reproach." But in the end they might be challenged to declare whom they would obey. This declaration of Jesus' lordship embodied subversive values. If there was a conflict of interest, they needed to declare, "We cannot keep from speaking about what we have seen and heard" (Acts 4:20); "We must obey God rather than any human authority" (Acts 5:29).

Jesus is Lord. We ascribe authority to Jesus. Whatever the New Testament context—worship, baptismal rites, or court scenes—this statement of allegiance rings out: "Jesus is Lord." Christian communities treasured and preserved the memory of their authoritative Lord. But what kind of authority was this? It was a rabbi's authority. No aspect of life was separated from it.

Did early Christian worship reflect this obedience to the authority of Jesus as Lord? Yes, we can see it in many instances. Jesus' disciples asked him to teach them to pray. They learned to reflect his piety, his intimacy with the Father, his concerns in prayer. Jesus gave them what might be better titled the "Disciples' Prayer," and in it they could closely follow his lead.

Jesus' own piety and prayer life were shaped by praying the Psalms. In this, too, the early Christians followed his way. In their common worship, they told and retold the stories of Jesus. This was an oral tradition that preserved eyewitness accounts. Special custodians of the story were called on to recount the tradition that had definitive authority for the church.

Jesus' way and his teachings pervade the epistles: "You are light. Live as children of light" (Eph. 5:8); "Let the same mind be in you that was in Christ Jesus" (Phil. 2:5); "Do not worry about anything" (Phil. 4:6); "And let the peace of Christ rule in your hearts" (Col. 3:15); Be "born anew" (1 Peter 1:23); "Even if you do suffer for doing what is right, you are blessed" (1 Pet. 3:14). The writers of these letters were Jesus' disciples! They recognized his authority. Jesus was Lord of their common life, their common prayer, and their praise.

Jesus' authoritative life and teachings, prayer, and piety shaped the lives of the early Christians. We see it in their creeds, in their Gospel proclamations, and in their teaching for baptism. Jesus himself was the core of their faith, experience, and worship. In the Gospels we find these rites—eucharist, baptism, foot washing—mandated by Jesus. His authoritative teaching shaped all the values and practices of their lives.

Jesus' authority in our worship

How does our worship embody and project the authority of Jesus as Lord? Sometimes I notice a tendency to argue with Jesus. "He didn't mean that!" "It doesn't apply now." I suggest that we take Jesus' words seriously, and as often as possible, incorporate them into our prayer and worship.

The words of the Lord's Prayer are probably the words of Jesus most often and regularly repeated in our worship. That is good. But when Jesus said to his disciples, "Pray like this," he might have meant more than simply to repeat the words he gave. Many Christians from the second century onward have used the prayer as an outline for their own extempore praying. Their free prayer follows the inner content and the outer pattern, beginning with the intimate address to Abba; the hallowing of God's name; moving on through prayer for kingdom concerns; thanks for bread and forgiveness; confession: and petition that we will be made into a forgiving people and kept safe from evil. In praying like this, we follow Jesus' deepest concerns and enter his fervent, loving relationship with the Father.

But there are other words of Jesus that we could also use. Because of their two-part form, the Beatitudes could easily become a regular part of worship. The first part of each one could be spoken, and the second part answered by the congregation. It could be done antiphonally between men and women.

We can memorize and use Jesus' blessings and words of comfort as conclusions of our confession prayers: "My peace I give to you. I do not give to you as the world gives" (John 14:27a). "Where are they? Has no one condemned you? . . . Go your way, and from now on do not sin again" (John 8:10-11). "Do not let your hearts be troubled and do not let them be afraid" (John 14:27b).

The great commandment lends itself to regular repetition as part of prayers of intercession or confession. It could be used to shape our prayers. It could order the whole of a worship service. It could also be used like this:

L: *Who do we love?*
P: *The Lord our God.*
L: *How do we love God?*
P: *With heart and soul, strength and mind.*
L: *Who do we love?*
P: *Our neighbors*
L: *How do we love them?*
P: *We love them as ourselves.*

We might also pray through John 17, remembering and reflecting on the passionate concèrns of Jesus. Are these the phrases and ideas that flood our spontaneous praying? If not, it is probably because we have not continuously listened to Jesus at prayer. What a privilege to have this text preserved for us! A moving dismissal blessing is to adapt Jesus' Nazareth manifesto like this. The whole congregation might memorize and say or sing it together.

The Spirit of the Lord is upon us, because he has anointed us to bring good news to the poor. He has sent us to proclaim release to the captives and recovery of sight to the blind. He has anointed us to let the oppressed go free. He has anointed us to proclaim (this year!) the year of the Lord's favor.

These days there are many exciting experiments with the retelling of Gospel stories—biblical storytelling, dynamic dramatizations, stories mimed and danced, rap stories. All of these help us keep Jesus' story alive in worship, and in doing so, keep his rabbinic, authoritative lordship in its proper place. His life, his words, and his stories have first place. Our own words take second place to his.

Many other texts spring to mind. John 3:16 and 17 are many people's favorite verses. How could we use them regularly in worship. Could we shape our prayers around them, sing them, paint them, or mime them? Perhaps we could name our services by the motto verses that mark out their themes: Instead of the time on the clock (the 9:30 service), we could call it the "Let the children come to me" service.

In all our praying, we can keep working to see things as Jesus saw them; to name things with his clarity; to expose our hypocrisy; to express grief at our sinfulness; to denounce the falsity of evil; to see the necessity for struggle for justice; and, above all, to honor the Father's merciful love.

Jesus is here

Jesus is here. In the weeks after the devastating event at Golgotha, Jesus unaccountably appeared to his frightened disciples, fully alive. In their assemblies, along the way, at table, and on the beach, suddenly Jesus was there. At first terrified and baffled, later on they came to understand and appropriate Jesus' promises to them: "I will ask the Father, and he will give you another Advocate, to be with you forever" (John 14:16). They explained their experience: "The Lord is the Spirit" (2 Cor. 3:17a).

In their worship the Lord was truly present! They worshiped and prayed in the power of the Spirit, through the Spirit. Though Acts reports that Christians attended temple prayers, for them the sacrificial cult had lost its meaning. Christians worshiped and prayed in homes, in settings similar to Jesus' post-resurrection appearances. Table companionship and the remembered meals with Jesus took on distinctive forms, because of Jesus' Last Supper with his disciples. All of these factors were newly significant.

But most important was the presence and operation of the Spirit. As they searched Scriptures and recalled Jesus' words to them, the Christians came to understand their experience in this way. In our life together, here, now, the prophets are vindicated. Their words are coming true. John the Baptist, Isaiah, Micah, Joel—it all fits together! It makes sense!

Now they remembered Jesus' own words: "The Spirit will remind you of all that I have said to you" (John. 14:26).

Everything Jesus had taught them the Spirit in retrospect now made clear: about the merciful Father, about God's kingdom, about love, about Jesus' arrest and execution, about his rising to life again. The meanings of all these things became their focus, gave identity to the community. No longer humiliated and afraid, they could now "proclaim the death of Christ." The whole story had to be told, interpreted, and celebrated. "Until he comes again!"

Worship to build up the church

The Spirit integrated the meaning of their faith and new life together. But as well, the Spirit's powerful presence brought their worship alive.

The only New Testament text that actually provides details about Christian worship is 1 Corinthians 14. To build up (edify) the community is the dominant image. In the course of this one chapter, we read of an astonishing variety of activities in the conduct of worship: tongues, revelation, prophecy, teaching (v. 6); saying a blessing, thanksgiving, "Amen," instruction (vv. 16-19, 24); hymn, lesson, revelation, interpretation of a tongue (v. 26). The purpose behind all of these varied, Spirited activities is clear in verse 26c: "Let all things be done for building up [the church]." In their worship all members took responsibility and contributed as they were enabled by the Spirit, whether in hymns, prayers, teachings, or any other ways the Spirit gave them. This was truly Spirit-animated worship.

Its decent orderliness had external impact as well, for missionary witness (v. 24). But through it all, the Spirit of Jesus animated and hovered; encouraged and lit the way for the common life and witness of the community. The Spirit of the Lord was the life of their worship.

Making space for the Spirit

This is true for us as it was for an early church community. The Spirit is active in all members' preparation for and expectation of worship. It's not just for the people up front. But worship leaders can enhance the expectation of the Spirit's presence and activity in worship. We can pray for receptiveness, for willingness to receive something fresh. Instead of rushing from one thing to the next, we can allow silence in our worship to listen to what the Spirit is saying.

We can reserve time at the close of worship for prayers of recapitulation, that is, a chance to hear again the significant words, phrases, thoughts, and pictures that may have arisen during worship. The Spirit may find a way to put these together for us in a step, a choice, or a conviction as we close our corporate worship. Do we encourage free expression, allow space for it to happen? Or do we show a lack of trust by trying to monitor and control everything? Do we give the appearance of freedom, and yet in reality rein in the Spirit and put things into our own order?

Charismatic Anabaptism

Anabaptism of sixteenth-century Europe was a Spirit movement. Anabaptist worship was charismatic, Spirit-inspired, and Spirit-energized. Its principles of practice were delineated in 1 Corinthians 14, just as we discussed above. Contributing to worship was every participant's responsibility. Each brought a hymn, a lesson, a revelation, or a prayer. People came prepared to take part.

Questions we might ask of our own Anabaptist-charismatic worship are: Does it build up the church? Does it give people their voice? Does it enhance their loving relationship to the Father? Does it develop the character of Jesus in individual members of the church? Does the character of the whole fellowship keep maturing, growing more loving, more peaceful, merciful, hospitable, and generous? Does the worship enable the church to reach out in love to the world around?

In our consumer age, we must even more urgently consider these questions. God has not called us to give people what they think they want—great music, a good nursery, youth clubs, emotional experiences, and entertainment. Do people want experience simply for its own sake? Do people come back just for the highs? Do we capitulate to modern worship fads or waves? Do we evaluate the effects of the nineteenth-century emotional legacy? Do we evaluate the effects of postmodern dynamics in today's society?

Jesus is the measure

"Jesus is here!" We worship on an immensely exciting, growing edge. Worship can be risky as well as inspiring. In worship we are listening, preparing ourselves, and expecting a word from God. Are we willing to appropriate that word for our lives, our lifestyle, as well as for our feelings? As we worship we look Jesus straight in the face, not in sideways glances! Jesus is here! "The Lord is here; his Spirit is with us!"

And so we see that the New Testament is a rich resource. It reveals much depth, though the evidence is fragmentary, about the worship of early Christian communities. It gives us words for worship. It evokes for us the spirit and ethos of worship. It gives advice and points to worship goals. We've considered three assertions about Jesus that the early Christians joyfully made. These assertions can serve as sight lines or landmarks to steer us as we worship.

Jesus is Messiah. Let's tell the great story of God, the saga of redemption and hope, and interpret our own time in its light. Jesus is Lord. Let's seek to worship so that we can inspire the walk of discipleship, strengthen our consciences, and soften our hearts. Jesus has authority in our lives. Let us develop the reflex of paying close attention to Jesus. He is Lord. Jesus is here. Through the Lord who is the Spirit, we pray, we discern, we worship. The Spirit energizes our lives individually and corporately. Life in the Spirit is for here and for now. Immanuel—God is with us!

So let us continue to express in our worship the simplicity, the truth, and the power of the gospel. We will find this in Jesus himself, the Lord of our worship. This Jesus Christ who is present in his Spirit, Lord and Messiah.

Chapter 2

An Anabaptist Perspective on Music in Worship

by John Rempel

Simply put, worship is the creature's response of gratitude and surrender to the goodness of the Creator. Worship is the never ceasing dramatization of the gospel; its major actors are God and the congregation. The order of worship carries forward the dialogue between God and us. We speak to one another on God's behalf and to God on one another's behalf. As she preaches, the preacher prays that God might make her words into God's word. The congregation responds in various ways, by entering a silence in which the seed of the word of God begins to sprout or with a hymn that echoes and amplifies the preacher's declaration of God's goodness.

In worship, we hear the promise of a new creation and taste its reality in time and space. In worship, fate and necessity are transcended, and we are placed in the realm of freedom. Therefore, we are able to embrace the world rather than merely enduring it. It is in this world we know with Paul that we are "perplexed but not driven to despair, . . . sorrowful, yet always rejoicing, . . . having nothing, and yet possessing everything" (2 Cor. 3:12—6:10, esp. 4:8 and 6:10). It is above all in worship that perplexity, sorrow, and poverty are deprived of finality; it is here that Jesus' conquest of the powers is made manifest. Jesus makes himself known in the gathering of believers; in the preaching of the word and the breaking of bread his victory becomes tangible.

For Christians, worship is not a private gathering of like-minded people; it is an event in which we participate because we have been given a relationship with one another through Jesus Christ. It is not, first of all, our sameness in experience, theology, or culture that unites us, but Christ's work on the cross of breaking down barriers and creating a new humanity (Eph. 2:14ff.). Those who lead worship do not do so as private individuals with private reasons for participating, but as representatives of the community; they act and speak on its behalf. Therefore, a gathering for worship needs to make room for all stages and conditions of human life. As Evelyn Underhill, the twentieth-century Christian mystic, so aptly put it, worship needs to find a place for elephants to swim and lambs to wade. Christian worship is corporate in its very essence: the fullness of the Spirit falls upon the gathered community; the fullness of the Word is heard there. In it, the broken bones of the body of Christ are reset and restored to health. Worship happens in many settings——in the serenity of a lakeside at dawn, in the fervor of a peace rally, in the intensity of a concert performance—but it is grounded in the weekly gathering of the church on the Lord's day around word and sacrament. This is not to say that worship is confined to the sacred assembly. It is truer to say that worship goes out from and comes back into that assembly. We disperse to pour out the cup of salvation for the world, then gather to replenish it. This is the natural rhythm of the church.

Worship is a ritual activity. In the free churches, we fear the word "ritual" because it connotes for us fixed forms in which we do not recognize our own voice. That is one kind of ritual. The essence of ritual is simple words and gestures that condense reality, stylize emotion, and act out memory. Ritual is fundamental to communication. Offering someone a handshake is a stylized but straightforward way of welcoming someone into our presence. It is accessible to people of different temperaments, even different languages. In ritual a simple action lets one in on a deeper reality. To take the most basic ritual of the church, the Lord's Supper, we believe that when we receive the communion bread, we also receive Christ.

Finally, Christian worship is worldly. We live in the flesh. God meets us as finite creatures in a fallen world. We do not have to rise above this world to find God. Pilgram Marpeck, a sixteenth-century Anabaptist theologian, never tired of repeating that "Christ became a natural man for natural men."[1] This means that our mortal nature is not a hindrance to but rather the means of God's presence in our lives. By extension, a musical score and the ritual pouring of water are bearers of grace.

The role of music in worship

Speech is ritual expression. With words we utter realities much bigger than these words. Yet it is by means of words that we share the experiences that shape our lives. To say to someone, "I love you," does not fully express my relationship to my beloved, but it does reveal my heart. Speech is the primal vehicle by which we move from isolation into encounter. Music is an accelerated mode of communication. When I listen to a Vivaldi cello concerto, my sense of being alive is heightened. Vocal music, specifically, is an indispensable extension of speech. It literally harmonizes individual voices into a collective sound. In that basic sense, music is sacramental: "It is a visible and outward sign of an invisible and spiritual grace" (Augustine).

Elie Wiesel recounts an incident in *Night*, his haunting autobiographical account of life in a concentration camp, which strikingly illustrates this truth. German soldiers drove thousands of starving prisoners through frigid winter weather. One day the survivors fell in exhaustion. Many died. Elie discovered that his friend Juliek was barely alive, with only one possession: his violin.

> *I heard the sound of a violin. The sound of a violin in this dark shed where the dead were heaped on the living. What madman could be playing the violin here at the brink of his own grave . . .? I could hear only the violin and it was as though Juliek's soul were the bow. He was playing his life. The whole of his life was gliding on the strings—his lost hopes, his charred past, his extinguished future.*[2]

In the notes of this fragment from a Beethoven concerto, Elie heard Juliek's soul.

It is not an exaggeration to claim that community can't be sustained without music. This is especially true of religious community where mystical realities beyond rational comprehension are poured into words. Yet the words are inadequate to express the truth they are trying to grasp. Music gives words wings. The musical expression of a truth enlarges it and makes possible a harmony of confession gathered together from different experiences and convictions. In my days as a college chaplain, I remember innumerable probings by clever minds into the meaning of theological statements. I recall a service in which, quite by chance, two faculty members and two students who were known for their challenging of traditional thought, had formed a quartet. I wondered what to expect from the mouths of these tireless questioners! In response to the sermon, they stood and sang with passionate intensity the pietistic chorale "What Mercy and Divine Compassion." In that moment their voices joined in the confession of the church across the centuries. Words were suddenly no longer earthbound and contentious; the music had borne them upward into a space great enough to include many fragmentary thoughts in one whole.

Even though music is the fount of creativity, it has

heeded the call to make itself the handmaiden of faith. Church music is the humblest—and by the same token perhaps the noblest—of the arts in that it lets itself be the vehicle, the servant, of the rhythms and truths of the gospel. Music in worship is functional in that it offers up its power to give life to the truths of the gospel. This is what Bach must have meant when he said that music exists for the glory of God.

The origins of Anabaptist worship

The Anabaptist criticism of worship in the church of the sixteenth century was above all that the people of God had lost their voice. Late medieval worship left the congregation without a participatory role and without words of its own. The service was conducted by the priest. (If there were other active participants, they were a choir speaking on behalf of the congregation.) The words and symbols of the official church—in Latin and in formulations reserved for the clergy—were so far removed as to be inaccessible to the masses of people.

Even then there were popular devotional movements which sought to make the people active participants in worship. These practices included the veneration of relics, the veneration of the eucharist outside of mass, and a preaching service accompanied by devotional songs called Prone. In the sixteenth century, Catholic and Protestant reformers alike continued the search for worship in which the people were actors. In some ways, Anabaptism was the most consistent and radical reform movement because it made the people the creators of their own worship. It stripped away set liturgical forms and gave ordinary people the confidence that the Holy Spirit would inspire worship in them.[3]

Given the above condition of worship and the resistance of the authorities to its reform, the extreme corrective Anabaptism brought to worship made pastoral, if not always theological, sense. The most extreme current of reform flowed through Zurich and found a home with both Zwingli and the Anabaptists. A little background helps us understand the impulse toward change. The cathedral in Zurich had a reputation for elaborate choral and instrumental music. Various sources speak of, for example, parts of the mass being set to elaborate polyphonic tunes, but also—amazingly—of replacing the words of the mass with frivolous secular texts sung in Latin in worship.[4] It was this state of musical affairs which led the Swiss reformers to reject, not only organs and choirs, but even congregational singing. In other parts of Europe, where liturgical music suffered less abuse, there were less extreme reactions; yet everywhere in Protestantism, but especially in Anabaptism, the cry was to put worship into the hands and voices of the congregation.

For Anabaptism, this meant novel media of worship like congregational singing and the interpretation of Scripture according to the insights of any believer, as well as the sharing of bread and wine like a family at table. Its practice of worship embraced both an openness to the immediate inspiration of the Spirit in spontaneous prayer and prophesying and also the creative adaptation of ancient actions like the Lord's Supper. What is noteworthy is that the congregation acted as a priesthood of believers, which meant, not only that the individual could come before God on her own behalf, but also that she came before God on behalf of her neighbor. Each believer was a mediator for the other. In his analysis of this development among the Swiss Brethren, J. F. G. Goeters describes their administration of the Lord's Supper as a movement from the self-communion of a priest without a congregation to the self-communion of a congregation without a priest.[5]

In most regions where Anabaptism flourished, congregational singing emerged as spontaneously as did prayer and Bible study. It measured the heartbeat of Anabaptist spirituality. Not only were hymns borrowed, great numbers of them were written. The earliest evidence of hymn writing is that of Anabaptist prisoners in the 1540s who comforted and exhorted one another with simple texts of their own writing or adapting and with tunes borrowed from popular culture. Many of these were gathered into the *Ausbund*, which was first published for Swiss and South German Anabaptists in 1564. Parallel developments among the Dutch and North German Anabaptists led to the publication of *Het Offer des Heeren*, another hymnal of martyr songs first published in 1562. A steady stream of hymnals followed between the 1560s and the 1630s, many of them compiled by leading ministers of the day like Hans de Ries, Leonard Clock, and Tilman van Braght.[6]

Two complementary changes took place in this same period of time. Gradually the role of the congregation in public prayer and Scripture interpretation came to an end. Preaching and praying was confined to ordained leaders. It should be remembered that there was always a plural ministry of ministers, deacons, and a bishop who regularly preached and presided. But the sad fact is that the voice of the people was confined again, as it had been for centuries in the old church, this time to the singing of hymns and the praying of the Lord's Prayer. Perhaps this limited role for congregational expression accounts for the amazing diversity in the early hymnbooks; they range from folk songs to psalms to chorales. What limited role the congregation had in carrying worship it did as fully as possible.

Orlando Schmidt observes that "the most important development during the centuries following the initial outburst of Anabaptist freedom was its formality."[7] Once the initial burst of dissent and creativity had shaped the Anabaptist movement, the overall concern in church life as well as in worship was the preservation of fixed expressions of beliefs and practices rather than the experience of the Spirit which had brought them about. Product was preferred to process. Renewal movements came upon the church at intervals in the succeeding centuries. Their most consistent feature was the borrowing and creating of new music as the voice of renewed piety. In a few of these renewals, most notably the early years of the Mennonite Brethren in Russia, aspects of the sixteenth-century pattern were recovered, and the people were invited to offer their own prayers in public and to join in the collective interpretation of Scripture. It was ultimately in missionary settings outside the North Atlantic world that the Mennonite Church recaptured the charismatic participation of the people in worship characteristic of early Anabaptism. In the homelands of Mennonitism, congregational participation continued to come solely through congregational singing. This state of affairs has slowly changed since the 1960s in North America, through the influence of the charismatic movement on one side of our church and the liturgical movement on the other, as well as through the emerging multicultural identity of mainstream Mennonitism. We are rightly pleased with the fact that on a given Sunday in North America, Mennonites worship in twenty languages and twenty ways.

The theology and practice of Anabaptist worship

Worship develops by means of what one might call a "liturgical circle." People come to faith, enter the church, and grasp a vision of the kingdom of God. This reality comes to expression through old and new forms. In the same congregation, for example, a new believer might be baptized to the accompaniment of Scripture songs and receive his first communion bread on a clean handkerchief he was asked to bring along for the occasion. Such developments are then reflected on theologically, made part of a new combination of customs, and then broken open again by new manifestations of the Spirit. It is not a matter of first arriving at an adequate theology of worship and then systematically putting it into effect. The dynamic nature of Christian worship is such that practice and reflection continually follow one another. Worship always bursts the bounds we set for it. It is more often in the doing of worship that we are led to its truth than in our abstract thoughts about it. In all probability the early church was bewildered by Jesus' command to break bread in remembrance of him. It was only in the doing of this action that they realized the presence of Christ in their midst. Sometimes the interchange between form and freedom leads to the incorporation of spontaneous responses into set liturgical reforms. Apparently the vibrant dancing that accompanies the liturgy of the Ethiopian Orthodox Church began as a spontaneous accompaniment to the order of service and gradually became a new expression of it.[8]

Out of this liturgical circle in which practice and reflection follow each other, at least six assumptions emerged to provide a foundation for Mennonite worship. First, those who respond in worship are Christ's sisters and brothers, believers who have confessed their own faith and been baptized. When we worship we are speaking from the heart. The words of the Bible, of hymns, and of prayers become our own, whether they are original formulations or pieces of tradition which come alive to the ear of faith. We find our own voices rather than having words put in our mouths.

Second, our worship is free in that it is not regulated by the state or fixed in any final form. We begin with the voice of tradition, but it is an open tradition that is expanded every time the community meets.

Third, our worship is ethical. The praise of God is not a means to a greater end, yet true praise always overflows into willing sacrifice.

Fourth, only God and people are holy in and of themselves. Times like the church year and places like meetinghouses take on meaning to the extent that they tell the story of salvation. The places we build and the times we set aside are signs of a presence that is near but cannot be contained. With this stipulation, ordinary objects can become signs of

God's nearness. At the first Anabaptist baptism on a farm near Zurich, for example, a water dipper and a bucket were brought from the kitchen to baptize, and an ordinary goblet and table wine became the stuff of communion.[9]

Fifth, worship is worldly. In the resurrection of Christ, God was victorious over evil in this world and this age. To worship God is to serve the groaning creation that waits with anticipation for redemption (Rom 8:19-23).

Sixth, worship as often challenges our habits of faith as it confirms them. In many Mennonite settings, this role of challenging believers was reduced to the preacher's admonitions, but they were often an inducement to conform. True worship holds before us a vision of the church and the world as they might be and dares us to bring them about.

Visual and musical artists among Mennonites have sought precedents in the tradition for the place of creativity in worship and the spiritual life. They have often been disappointed in what they have found in a church that became word-centered early on and that was forced by persecution into isolation from and fear of the world. A more fruitful entry point in the Mennonite tradition for artistic expression is surely the dissenting creativity of the first Anabaptists and the places in the liturgical circle across the centuries at which the spiritual imagination broke new ground.[10]

The impression is sometimes given that openness to the Spirit and the use of common speech and forms in Mennonite tradition leave little room for the care and competence of someone trained in preaching, worship leading, or music. In other words, is there any room for the professional? Balthasar Hubmaier, a first-generation Anabaptist with an earned doctorate in theology, is an example of an accomplished liturgical writer and preacher who, nonetheless, placed his skills within the giftedness of the whole community. In his "Form for Christ's Supper," an order for communion from 1527, Hubmaier makes a place for two kinds of competence: one that grows out of spiritual receptiveness and one that comes from training and practice. For example, he urges the preacher to set forth "the boundless goodness of Christ," but he also sets down standards for preaching that are concerned, not just with natural talent or spontaneous inspiration, but also with theological and rhetorical standards. At the same time, he provides for a time after the sermon for anyone "to whom something is revealed" to teach the congregation. His model, as was widespread in Anabaptism, is the church in Corinth, especially as modeled in 1 Corinthians 12 and 14.[11]

The meaning of the Anabaptist tradition for worship today

Anabaptism deserves our emulation in its signal contribution to the Reformation of returning worship to the people. It gave them the confidence that they could understand and follow the Bible and that they were agents of the Holy Spirit. Its limitation was that it absolutized the corrective that it had brought to Christian worship. The surpassing need of the age in which Anabaptism was born was to know that God gives his Spirit to all believers and that he cannot be found in customs and rituals as if by magic. Today we live in another time. Sacramental and symbolic realities have become a fragile species. We do not have to fight off an interpretation of how Christ is present in the Lord's Supper, which overreaches itself, like transubstantiation; we need to make credible the claim that he does make himself known to us in the breaking of bread (Luke 24:35). In Western countries, signs of God are scarce; most of them have tumbled to the ground like the last leaves of autumn leaving a barren landscape. A confident faith in the ongoing work of the Spirit in unfolding the meaning of the Bible for our time makes us free to discern what is binding and what is passing in our part of the larger tradition of the church. This means that we hold ourselves accountable to Anabaptism as our model, but we are not obligated to perpetuate correctives which represented the gospel in the sixteenth century but do not speak to conditions today.

There remain striking parallels between society and church in the sixteenth century and today. The fact is often overlooked that Anabaptism allowed the world into the church in ways that institutionalized forms of renewal in Protestantism as well as Catholicism were unable to do. For instance, Anabaptism accepted the songs of popular culture, it legitimized ordinary speech—not just an elitist vernacular—and it dignified the common people with membership in the priesthood of Christ. These breaks with the past were imaginative acts of dissent prompted by the cries of the people for a new word from God. It is this spirit that can help us find new expressions of worship as an alternative to fossilized tradition and highbrow innovation. In making use of popular culture, Anabaptism did not do so uncritically. At its best moments, it challenged the hierarchy of clergy and magistrates prevalent in society and weaned popular religion from association with nationalism and militarism.

The meaning of music in Mennonite worship today

Two questions can guide our search for authentic forms of worship and the authentic use of music. The first is: What does it mean that worship is transformative, in other words, that praise overflows into self-sacrifice? How can music shape worship that believes that change of heart and change of society is possible? Second, what does it mean that worship is worldly or that worship and work are inseparable? A basic criterion then for the role of music in worship is its power to transform. By the notion of transformation, we mean more than an immediate emotional effect, a short-lived burst of sentiment. At the same time, music leads us to an emotional receptivity to the things of God. It can free us to make decisions that might otherwise be out of our reach. We come to worship blinded to the neighbor before our eyes. We leave worship with eyes and hands of compassion.

I continue to be amazed at the range of musical and worship styles that can dispose us to waiting on God. A few years ago, I attended the service of the most traditional Old Colony Mennonite congregation (so I was told) in southern Manitoba. The service was entirely in German and followed traditional form in all its details. When the first song leader announced without flourish but with evident intensity the opening hymn, *"Komm, Heiliger Geist"* (Come, Holy Spirit), a sixteenth-century chorale in chant form, the congregation burst into song. Very soon thereafter, I attended our local New York Mennonite convention, which is made up of people from many cultures and races. The opening hymn on that occasion was "My Life's Found in You, Lord," a bright and rhythmic contemporary song, introduced and sung with many flourishes. Yet, the air of expectancy, the yearning for a word from God in the one service was markedly similar to that of the other.

What specific lessons can we draw from Mennonite tradition for the practice of church music? One is that the congregation is the basic actor in worship. This means that hymn singing is the basic carrier of worship. Often this will be brought about by means of previously chosen hymns which carry the movements of worship forward, but where there is a common repository of hymns, spontaneous requests in response to the flow of worship can be meaningful. Vocal and instrumental music can, however, represent the congregation before God just as the preacher does. One of the unique roles of vocal and instrumental music is that they can offer a stylized response to a preceding reading or prayer which expresses the experience of the worshipers but could not have been articulated by them spontaneously with such immediacy.

Two architectural proposals flow from these assumptions. One of them is that the congregation that sees itself as a priesthood of believers should be seated around the

Lord's table, which should be in the center of the church. Those who serve by leading should not be the only ones worshipers see face-to-face. In the traditional rectangular Mennonite meetinghouse style dominant until the beginning of this century, the congregation sat on three sides facing one another, and the leaders sat as a group on the fourth side. In some of these churches, the Lord's table dominated the center of the room.[12] It was the space where communion and even foot washing happened! The immediate response of most preachers and musicians to this disruptive proposal is that existing churches cannot be so rearranged. Let me challenge that assumption with an example. Some years ago, I visited the French village of La Ciotat, and took time to visit the local Roman Catholic church. It was a sixteenth-century, late-Gothic building with a long nave. The congregation had completely reshaped that space by placing a prominent Lord's table in the center and arranging rows of chairs all around, one section of which was reserved for the choir. I knew the moment I beheld this church that it was the perfect architectural expression of a Mennonite theology of worship. If the Catholics can do it, why can't we?

It is worth noting that when choirs were first accepted in Mennonite worship in Russia in the late nineteenth century, they were almost always placed in the second-floor balcony rather than on the ground floor at the front of the church. Historically, this has been the preferred location for choirs and instruments in the liturgical churches as well.

When choirs and other vocal or instrumental ensembles were first accepted by free churches in worship, they were a liturgical intrusion. What I mean by this startling statement is the following: Because the service was carried forward by a functional progression of hymn, prayer, Scripture reading, sermon, prayer, and hymn, music by people other than the whole congregation did not have an obvious function.[13] At its worst, "special" music became a decoration or diversion. It was often prepared without reference to the church year or the theme of the service. This has completely changed in most mainstream congregations. The principle at issue is that each aspect of the service is important in and of itself but equally for its capacity to carry forward our encounter with God. Understood in its strictest sense, this would mean that service music would need to move the service, for example, from a confession of sin to an expression of praise. I understand the role of choirs and instruments less narrowly, though still as a servant of the service. But there needs to be room for music that is part of the service because it has the capacity to show forth the beauty of God. How does one make room for outbursts of praise that nevertheless remain within the shape of the liturgy?

The task of shaping and leading worship is unending. But so is the presence of the Spirit and the wisdom of the church of many ages. Let us begin with the confession that our words and our melodies are seldom adequate to express the greatness of God. But let us not shrink from the call to lead worship. Like every other spiritual engagement, it is not only an occupation—in which one's technical competence is all that counts—but also a gift and a desire to be worthy of the gift. By knowing and having affection for Scripture and tradition, by staying close to the Holy Spirit in our preparations, then holding lightly to them, so that we can also seize the moment, we inspire those around us to do likewise. We prepare for the time of worship, but we cannot fully anticipate it. If we do not try to domesticate the Spirit, our worship will somehow always be more than we have rehearsed.

ENDNOTES

1. William Klassen and Walter Klaassen, *The Writings of Pilgram Marpeck* (Kitchener, Ont., and Scottdale, Pa.: Herald Press, 1978), 85.

2. Elie Wiesel, *Night* (New York: Avon Books, 1969), 107.

3. Shem Peachey and Paul Peachey, "Answer of Some Who Are Called . . . (Ana)Baptists," *Mennonite Quarterly Review* 45 (1971): 5-32 interprets 1 Corinthians 14 as the foundation of worship and measures orthodoxy by this practice.

4. Charles Garside, *Zwingli and the Arts* (New Haven: Yale University, 1966), 45f.

5. J. F. G. Goeters, ed., *Studien zur Geschichte und Theologie der Reformation* (Newkirchen: Neukirchener, 1969), 270.

6. Walter H. Hohmann, *Outlines in Hymnology* (North Newton, Kan.: Bethel College, 1941), 23f.

7. Orlando Schmidt, *Church Music and Worship Among the Mennonites* (Newton, Kan.: Faith and Life, 1981), 18.

8. I am indebted to John Plummer for this train of thought.

9. Fritz Blanke, *Brothers in Christ* (Scottdale: Herald Press, 1962), 22ff.

10. Conversation with Abner Hershberger was valuable in arriving at this insight.

11. H. Wayne Pipkin and J. H. Yoder, eds., *Balthasar Hubmaier: Theologian of Anabaptism* (Kitchener and Scottdale: Herald Press, 1989), 395, 396f.

12. Alastair Hamilton, et al., *From Martyr to Muppy* (Amsterdam: Amsterdam University, 1994), 12, 27, 39. Contemporary prints of worship gatherings illustrate a variety of space usages.

13. Harold M. Best, "Philosophy of Music in Free Church Worship," in *The Complete Library of Christian Worship*, vol. 4, book 1, R. Webber, ed. (Nashville: Star Song, 1994), 125f. H. Best has an insightful discussion of this problem in free churches.

Chapter 3

Crossing the Border: Music as Traveler

by Bernie Neufeld

My travels in Colombia, South America; eight countries in Europe; the United States; and various provinces within Canada have offered me the opportunity to participate in numerous worship services. To adequately represent the shape, the function, or the spirit of any individual service, and the role that music plays in the service would be impossible. What I would like to do is to consider the metaphor "music as traveler" as a window through which to look at the ministry of music in worship.

Crossing physical borders conjures up mixed feelings and experiences. In Canada, unless there is a flagrant disregard for the laws of the land, one can readily traverse the length and the breadth of the country without fear, and, yes, without interference from any form of authority. We can travel from Pacific Ocean to Atlantic Ocean, a distance of more than 5000 kilometers, without check stops. The only reminder that a border has been crossed is a sign identifying the name of the province. Crossing the border from one country to another does, however, entail some challenges. Customs offices, which require proper identification, information about country of birth, amount of money spent, in some instances the kind of product purchased, and questions about a criminal record are just some of the challenges that may come into question when crossing the border. Some country crossings are indeed very difficult and may in fact prove to be dangerous.

What does border crossing have to do with music in worship? First, the image of the traveler experiencing different situations, depending on the nature of the boundary crossing, can be helpful to the person giving leadership to music in worship. Consider the following:[1]

Traveling enhances learning and sharing

All of us come out of a particular culture and that culture determines to a large degree how we think and act. Traveling to different countries and experiencing those cultures broadens our horizons and allows us to reflect on experiences in ways not considered before. Similarly, our understanding of worship may be enhanced as we listen to, watch, and participate in the various activities that occur during the time of worship in different worship services.

Certainly, many choir conductors, pastors, and other church leaders have had experiences which are similar to mine; namely, that as one attends worship services, seminars, concerts, etc., in other places, ideas and information are often shared. Encounters in places other than one's home environment can often rekindle the flame that sometimes tends to flicker or indeed is snuffed out through weariness or lack of creative energy.

A memorable experience which confirmed this for me occurred in London, England, at the Wood Green Mennonite Church where I was fortunate to be present at the celebration of the congregation's twentieth anniversary. This small but vibrant group of people read Scripture, sang, prayed, preached, and shared of God's faithfulness. A fellowship meal brought the celebrations to a fitting close. What was particularly uplifting in this experience was that the worship music included the familiar and the new. I could on the one hand claim "tradition" (I am part of something that has been there for a long time), and on the other hand, I could experience a "new song." It is this "new song" that offers freshness and keeps us from going stale.

Traveling helps to build relationships

My own personal travels have taken me to numerous settings where the events planned were of an ecumenical nature. Being present and participating in worship, seminars, and workshops organized and planned by Catholics, Lutherans, Methodists, United Church, and other faith traditions were of immense benefit to me. Mingling with persons of varied faith persuasions breaks down barriers and consequently strengthens relationships. I find it to be wonderfully reassuring to know that we all worship the same God; that we have a common faith through Christ Jesus; that we share a common repertoire of hymnody and choral literature; and that many of my concerns are also the concerns of my fellow music travelers.

In 1996 I had the privilege, along with a dozen other Mennonite educators from North America, of visiting Mennonite churches in Bogotá, Colombia, and the surrounding area. Our very first visit was to a small congregation outside of Bogotá. We were on our way to a Mennonite retreat center but decided to make a picture stop at the church. To our surprise, the entire congregation was waiting for us to arrive. In fact, they had expected us one hour earlier. In the meantime, they were singing hymns and spiritual songs. The moment we stepped into the building, we had the sense that something quite unusual was about to happen. During a time of conversation, it seemed as though we had known each other for a lifetime. Sharing our faith and stories with one another was an incredibly moving experience. This was a small struggling congregation, but the lasting impression that will remain with me, and I know it was the same for the rest of our group, had to do with the manner in which these people sang their faith. From a professional musician's point of view, everything was wrong. The enthusiastic song leader sang loudly in a different key from that which was being played on the keyboard. Whom were we to follow? The person playing the tambourine played a different rhythm than the other two musicians. The congregation meanwhile sang with a zeal rarely heard before by this writer, yet it seemed as though the Spirit of God was at work. It is difficult to describe what happened that evening, except to say that the two Scripture passages quoted in the preface to this book took on a totally different meaning; it was a truly humbling and blessed experience. The food prepared and offered to us by the congregation at the conclusion of our visit was the capstone to a remarkable encounter with God, the congregation, and our tour group.

Welcoming the traveler

The metaphor "music as traveler" has another side to it. I have stressed how invaluable it can be to go beyond one's own borders to gather new insights and to become re-energized. Equally important, yet often sadly lacking, is an openness on the part of our congregations to accept a traveler into our midst. Yes, we may indeed welcome the person with a most generous spirit, but do we welcome the ideas and experiences and this person's song into our worship? Many of our congregations have been active in supporting refugee programs. In the past twenty years, we have assisted Laotian refugees, people from war-torn African countries, people from Central America, and most recently persons from Bosnia. These people also have a song. Their song has been their source of strength and hope as they have coped with life and death in often very trying circumstances. Do we expect these travelers coming to worship service after worship service to sing only our song? Can the song of the traveler coming from another culture find expression within the North American Mennonite congregation? This remains a major challenge.

The shape of worship: The function of the worship planning committee

Many congregations have chosen to delegate the planning of worship to a worship committee, rather than to one person, which in many instances has been the pastor. I believe this direction is commendable if the following broad guidelines are observed:

1. The pastor is considered by the congregation to be the spiritual leader and as such brings to the table themes, issues, etc., that will help shape the faith journey of the parishioner. This does not prevent others in the planning committee from submitting themes and ideas to complement and augment those of the pastor.

2. The worship planning committee is the voice that represents the congregation.

3. The worship planning committee is a sounding board for the pastor.

4. Since music plays a prominent role in most congregations, a person from the music committee is represented on the worship planning committee. Some congregations have merged these two into one committee.

Being any more specific would limit the individual congregation in addressing its own particular needs. What is important is for everyone to note that planning for worship is the most awesome and responsible task given to a congregation, for we are about the business of worshiping God. Worship planning is not to be treated as an exercise or a competition; rather, it calls forth the planners to lead the congregation toward a more faithful walk with God in their daily living.

Worship styles

From the discourse that Jesus had with the woman at the well as a result of her question regarding the proper place to worship,[2] we gather that it is not important to ask **where** or **how** we worship but **who** and **why** we worship. Some churches sincerely struggle with these questions. Often, though, churches tend to be guided by "successful" neighboring churches, the latest fad or trend that comes from religious television broadcasts, or aggressive marketing agencies pushing their particular brand of music or theology. The struggle is a difficult one, and it is ongoing.

There has been an explosion of worship materials, both from denominational and non-denominational quarters, in recent years. Practically every denomination has produced a new hymnal within the past five years, and the situation is similar in other worship resourcing. My personal bias is to plan and act out worship within the parameters of the Mennonite Church. One realizes that although each congregation within the larger framework has its own individual identity, and therefore makes independent decisions, there is nonetheless a connectedness to the larger body. That often translates into doing and saying things in worship that reflect our common way of living out our faith.

Robert Webber claims that in our Western world there are, broadly speaking, seven styles of morning worship: (1) liturgical, (2) traditional Protestant, (3) creative, (4) charismatic, (5) praise and worship tradition, (6) convergence, and (7) the seekers' service/believers' worship pattern.[3] Currently we are also hearing about the vineyard tradition. Historically, Mennonites have worshiped in a free church tradition; that is, since the sixteenth-century Reformation, Mennonites have stressed freedom from ritual requirements. Major emphasis is placed on preaching/teaching the Word (proclamation); however, what is equally important is the living out of that Word. This living out of the Word has been called "discipleship." As in other faith traditions, many changes have occurred in Mennonite worship since the early 1960s. *Hymnal: A Worship Book*[4] has been a welcome resource in many Mennonite congregations as the structure of the book provides a model for an order of worship. This hymnal is much more inclusive in its imagery, language, hymns of various cultures, and styles of songs than previous hymnbooks have been.

It should be stated clearly from the outset that, whereas in the past one could expect reasonably similar patterns of worship within North American Mennonite churches, this is no longer as predictable today. Most of the seven worship styles, or components thereof, which Webber refers to are variously represented in Mennonite churches. What has led to this diversification of worship styles? Greater participation by lay people in providing leadership, more participation by the entire church body, and autonomy of individual churches are some of the more recent changes.

In many churches a worship planning committee looks ahead six months to a year, or even longer, to ensure that important events such as Thanksgiving and Pentecost are taken into account and that there is a balance in the content of the services. A welcome addition to planning worship is the use of the lectionary, a three-year worship tool organized according to the Christian church calendar year. The lectionary, which includes Scripture passages and related themes, ensures that the entire Bible, instead of only favorite passages, is utilized in the reading in worship. The use of this worship tool as a directive also gives musicians the opportunity to do more long-range planning.

Giving shape to five worship services

Mennonite churches no longer consist of only white, middle-class members with European ancestry. Our congregations are made up of people who come from very diverse backgrounds; the color of skin, language, dress, cultural values, and a myriad of other characteristics reveal our differences. How can Paul's words *to live in harmony with one another, in accordance with Jesus Christ, so that together you may with one voice glorify God the Father of our Lord*

Jesus Christ[5] bring about unity in the midst of so much diversity in our worship? By addressing five different styles of worship, I hope to lead us to a greater understanding of why we do what we do in our worship. The goal is not to promote one style over and against another, rather, it is to help planners of worship to become more conscious of **who** it is that is being worshiped, **who** it is that comes to worship, and **how**, with greater understanding, the full message of God's revelation through Jesus Christ can be brought to all humankind.

Example 1: Isaiah 6:1-9

- *God is revealed* (vv. 1-4): God is the object of our worship. The words and symbols we use and the music we offer all usher us into the presence of the transcendent God. This may take the form of: a call to worship (sung or spoken); a prayer of invocation; Scripture reading; words of welcome; choir ministry; congregational singing, etc.

- *Confession* (v. 5): In comparison to God, humans are lost and sinful. We need to confess "our uncleanness" before God. Music, litanies, prayers, etc., can lead us into a purposeful time of confession. The tone of our music making will no doubt take on a different character than in other sections. In this section one might consider: prayer (spoken/sung); sharing by the people; Scripture reading by a leader or a responsive reading, possibly based on Psalm 51; congregational hymns of confession.[6]

- *Forgiveness/reconciliation* (vv. 6-7): The One who is so wondrously revealed to us hears our confessions and forgives our sins. We become reconciled to God. Appropriate prayers, songs,[7] and symbols of gratitude could be offered here.

- *Calling/proclamation* (v. 8a.): The call goes out to the believer to go into the world to proclaim the good news. This may be done in the form of a sermon/meditation; however, the Word may be expounded on in any one of the sections, or the message can be split up into several parts and included in various sections. The components of the proclamation might also include: a children's feature; additional Scripture readings; choir anthem; sermon; congregational response (hymn) to the message; sharing by members; prayer. A congregational response is a good way to complete this section.

- *Sending/commitment* (vv. 8b-13): Having experienced forgiveness and healing, the believer is ready to be a faithful witness as he or she goes out into the world. This may take the form of: displaying or handing out a concrete symbol that visually helps us to better remember the theme; sharing and announcements; taking the offering; prayer; music ministry; congregational song; benediction. A handshake with the persons around you, wishing them the "peace of God" or a similar blessing might be an appropriate way to complete the sending.

Hymns or songs and other forms of music ministry should be inserted appropriately into the above sections. To facilitate the reality that people coming to worship have different musical backgrounds, every effort should be made by the leaders to create a balance of musical styles. Unfortunately, some congregations insist on using only older hymnals. These older hymnals do not reflect the numerous changes that are taking place in music publication. Neither do they reflect societal changes in general that impact the life of the congregation. Could it be that churches that refuse to purchase the newer hymnals will find themselves swinging over entirely to the singing of contemporary songs? That would be a mistake! I believe the leaders of the church should ensure that both the familiar (which is normally contained in hymnals) and the new (which to some degree finds its way into new or revised hymnals), plus other contemporary styles which do not appear in hymnals, are needed to keep the faith community together.

Example 2: Suggested order in *Hymnal: A Worship Book*
- *Gathering*
- *Praising/adoring*
- *Confession/reconciliation*
- *Proclamation*
- *Witness/service*
- *Sending*

This order found in the table of contents is similar in function to example 1 in being supportive of the Word. Similar procedures in regard to music ministry choices apply in planning the order of worship.

Example 3: The Taizé tradition[8]

The Taizé Community is an ecumenical Christian community in France begun by Brother Roger in the early 1940s. Thousands of young people, young adults, and adults gather here every year for community worship, Bible study, and personal spiritual reflection. According to George Carey, Archbishop of Canterbury,[9] Taizé teaches us four things: (1) that young people respond to warmth and affection; (2) that we need to value the qualities and insights which young adults bring to church life; (3) that we are to be participants rather than spectators; and (4) that young people and young adults respond to genuine spirituality. What follows is the structure of a typical Taizé worship service or "prayer time" as it is often referred to. The reader should note that most of the newer hymnals have some songs originating from the Taizé Community.

- *Opening songs* (usually two meditative songs): People gather in body and spirit to deepen the sense of meditation through common song.
- *Alleluia and psalm:* The cantor chants a psalm in sections, and the congregation responds with the "alleluia" after each section.[10]
- *A song of light* (optional): This is the time where children may be involved by lighting a candle to symbolize

that even when we are surrounded by darkness in our own personal lives, Christ's love is a fire that never goes out.

- *Bible reading:* The Bible reading is not long and stands on its own without any explanation.

- *Song:* A meditative song that introduces a period of silence.

- *Silence* (five to ten minutes): Some soft background music **may** be used. A fairly long period of silence to listen to the voice of God deep within is essential in discovering the heart of prayer.

- *Prayers of intercession or adoration:* Different persons lead out with **short** prayers of intercession or thanksgiving. A Kyrie[11] or other suitable response is sung after each petition is spoken.

- *The "Our Father" (the Lord's Prayer) and a concluding prayer.*

- *Concluding songs:* The prayer before ends on a peaceful note. The concluding songs are again of a meditative nature. People leave the sanctuary at will.

Singing is very important in Taizé worship. The songs are usually short, chant-like, with few words, and are repeated again and again.

Example 4: A charismatic worship format[12]

As in other worship styles, charismatic worship varies from congregation to congregation or for that matter from service to service within one congregation.

Half an hour before the service begins, the musicians (often two guitarists, a pianist, and a drummer) begin to play the music of charismatic worship: folk-like songs and songs of devotion and praise. Various expressions of greeting are made as people enter into worship.

- *Prayers of adoration and praise* (occupies the first third of the worship service): They can take the form of: singing the Psalms and other Scripture; uttering brief offerings of adoration; reading or reciting passages of Scripture that exalt the triune God, sometimes with brief comments of personal praise; praying set prayers from a prepared liturgy or led by appointed lay persons or pastors; dancing, spontaneous or carefully choreographed and prepared as an offering of praise; enacting prayer in other ways—bowing, kneeling, standing with raised hands.

- *Prayers of confession:* These may be sung, spoken, or silent—spontaneous or planned. The prayers are often enacted in various ways: they may be read to each other or read together; they may be written prayers that can be burned in the flame of a candle. Candles may be lit—often followed by exclamations of praise: "Our sins are forgiven in Christ!"

- *Prayers of thanksgiving:* Brief expressions of gratefulness in the form of Scripture readings, singing, material gifts, or gifts of talents are given. Sharing of how God has guided people in daily life would also be part of this section of worship.

- *Prayers of intercession and of supplication:* (This may take up the second third of the usual worship time.) Prayers may consist of the following: spoken requests or petitions, praying "in the Spirit," and praying in smaller groups. A healing service may form part of the service and listening to the Spirit and to the prayers of other persons are key elements of worship. The Lord's Supper, often preceded by the divine healing act, fills a significant role in charismatic worship.

- *Climax:* A service of commissioning for special acts of ministry to the local community and beyond takes place at this time. Prayers of commitment to discipleship are spoken, and the congregation affirms these persons by the act of laying on of hands.

Song plays an important role in charismatic worship. Melicent Huneycutt Vergeer describes the role of music this way:

*Much of the prayer so central to charismatic worship is
expressed in song. Spontaneous music is apt to burst forth at any
point in the service as an expression of praise, joy and thanksgiving, or need.*[13]

Although most of the music associated with charismatic worship is in the style of Scripture songs, which lend
themselves to greater spontaneity, Vergeer reminds us that
worship hymns of the ages, like "Holy, Holy, Holy" and
"O Worship the King," are also sung. Contrary to most
Mennonite and mainline denominational churches, charis-
matics believe in the involvement of the whole person.
Clapping hands, raising arms, snapping fingers, moving
and dancing in the aisles, and swaying to the music give
vibrancy to the singing.

Example 5: A seekers' service/believers' worship

According to Webber,[14] the seekers' service replaces the
typical Sunday morning worship, whereas the believers'
worship is conducted during the week or on Sunday
evening. The church most frequently referred to in connection with seekers'/believers' worship is the Willow Creek
Community Church in suburban Chicago. Normally, the
Sunday morning service is reserved for the nonthreatening
presentation of the gospel. The claim is that many people
are disenchanted with the traditional church for the following reasons: churches are constantly asking for money;
the preaching is unrelated to daily living; and the worship
forms used are pointless and out of touch with contemporary society. As a response then, the seekers' church pro-
motes itself to the public as a church where people can
come and enjoy the service or simply listen; they are not
expected to come dressed in Sunday clothes, to give
money, or to participate in the singing of congregational
songs. They are in a real sense watching a performance, a

performance that is very professional. This professionalism is evident in all of the stage activity, from the sermon to the orchestra/vocal team/ solo/ensemble music. The central feature is the sermon, which tends to not be heavy on Bible or theology, but rather to emphasize the relevance of the Christian faith for daily contemporary living.

Believers' worship is conducted during the week and/or Sunday evening. This service consists mainly of singing (praise and worship style) plus instruction and a monthly celebration of the Lord's Supper. Believers (members) are organized into cell groups for prayer, Bible study, fellowship, ministry, and service, and usually meet in these groups weekly.

The seekers' pattern of worship might take the following shape:[15]

- *Prelude*: The band plays upbeat music as people enter the place of worship.

- *Welcome*: One of the vocal team members welcomes the people and then leads in a short chorus that is printed in the bulletin or projected onto an overhead screen.

- *Vocal duet*: The duet focuses on the theme of the message. The singers are accompanied by the band.

- *Drama*: The group tries to inject humor into the drama while the drama itself centers on the theme of the morning.

- *Scripture*: Based on the theme.

- *Song*: This song is performed and accompanied by the band.

- *Announcements*: Only announcements relevant to a seeker are made.

- *Offering*: Seekers are explicitly told they do not need to contribute to the offering.

- *Message*: The message lasts approximately thirty minutes and focuses on the theme of the service. As described earlier, the preacher will target the seeker mentality and will deliver the sermon with clarity and contemporary illustrations.

- *Discussion and fellowship*: People leaving the worship

are encouraged to enter into a period of discussion in the context of Christian fellowship.

*Different worship styles as outlined above are not ends in themselves but are used to address perceived needs. They can serve to guide the gathered people through worship experiences. Ultimately, our goal must always be: to *worship God in Spirit and in truth* and *together . . . with one voice* [to] *glorify the God and Father of our Lord Jesus Christ.*[16]

A hymn festival

Today we experience a tremendous diversity of musical styles and tastes. We are being challenged to learn new hymns and songs while singing the familiar and to draw persons of all ages (vocalists/instrumentalists/song leaders/readers, etc.) into participation in worship. One way of creatively responding to all these challenges is to plan a hymn festival as a Sunday morning worship service. Many communities and churches that have programmed these services have sensed a greater vitality in the singing and experienced the educational dimensions of such an endeavor. I will include one example of such a service planned in my home congregation. A brief warning: this type of service takes much hard work, and planning must begin far in advance of the event. All hymns in this hymn festival are taken from *Hymnal: A Worship Book* unless otherwise noted.

TO GOD BE THE GLORY
and
"may the congregation be encouraged to sing 'psalms, hymns, and spiritual songs'— both familiar and new"

A Hymn Festival, " . . . through the church the song goes on"

Opening Hymns	*Holy God, We Praise Thy Name*[17]

(ww. quartet, choir, cong./org.)

sts. 1, 2, &, 4	parts
st. 3	unison

Holy Lord (sung to the tune of "Dona Nobis Pacem")

1x	choir
2x	all
3x	3-part round

Introduction

God's Work in Creation

Narration

Hymns *All Things Bright and Beautiful* (w. children)

sts. 1, 2 &, 4	parts
st. 3	unison

For the Beauty of the Earth

sts. 1 & 5	parts
st. 2	women
st. 3	all, unison
st. 4	men

The Fall (confession)—The Covenant

Narration

Hymns *Aus tiefer Not schrei ich zu dir*
(Gesangbuch der Mennoniten)

sts. 1-3	parts

We Give Thanks unto You

sts. 1-5	soloist & congregation

Choir *More Precious Than Gold*

Exodus from Egypt

> Narration
> Hymn   *Children of the Heavenly Father*
> > > sts. 1 & 4   parts
> > > st. 2   men
> > > st. 3   women

Longing for the Savior

> Narration
> Hymns   *They That Wait upon the Lord*
> (sax / guitar / piano)
> > > 1x   saxophone
> > > 2 & 3x   all sing
> *O Come, O Come Immanuel* (a cappella)
> > > st. 1   choir
> > > sts. 2 & 6   all

The Savior Has Come

> Hymns   *Hark! The Glad Sound* (flute / piano)
> > > st. 1   choir
> > > sts. 2 & 3   all
> *Nun ist sie erschienen*
> *(Gesangbuch der Mennoniten)*
> > > sts. 1 & 2   all

The Ministry of Jesus

> Song   *Lord, You Have Come to the Lakeshore*
> (piano / guitar / flute)
> > > st. 1   solo
> > > sts. 2 & 4   all
> Reading   "He Was in the World"
> written by John Bell[18]
> Song   *Blessed Are the Persecuted* (drum)
> > > st. 1   choir
> > > st. 2   all, unison
> > > sts. 3 & 4   all—in parts

The Passion of Jesus

Narration
Hymns

Herzliebster Jesu (Gesangbuch der Mennoniten)
  sts. 1-3 parts
There Is a Green Hill Far Away (Mennonite Hymnal)

st. 1 & 2	all
st. 3	women
st. 4	men
st. 5	all, unison

The Resurrection of Jesus

Song

Come, Ye Faithful, Raise the Strain (piano, a cappella)

st. 1	choir
st. 2	all in parts
st. 3	all, unison

Reading

"We Met Him at the Close of Day" written by John Bell[19]

Song

I Am the Bread of Life (piano / guitar)

st. 1	men
st. 4	women
st. 5	all

A Faith That Will Endure

Narration
Hymns

When Peace, Like a River

st. 1	reflect as organ is being played
sts. 2, 3, & 4	all in parts

Nada te turbe (Let Nothing Trouble You) (organ / flute / oboe / vocal soloists)

1x	choir
2-7x	all

Look Around—Near and Far

Narration

Hymns
God Loves All His Many People
(piano / guitar / a cappella)

	st. 1	solo
	sts. 2 & 3	all

Will You Let Me Be Your Servant
(organ / guitar / a cappella)

	sts. 1, 2, & 6	parts
	st. 3	men
	st. 4	women
	st. 5	all unison

The Church Goes On

Reading
"We Did Not Want to Go"
written by John Bell[20]
(Testimony of four followers of Christ)

Hymn
Renew Your Church (piano / organ)

	sts. 1-3	in parts

Offering (in silence)

Congregational prayer

Announcements

Hymn

(benediction)
May the Grace of Christ
(Mennonite Hymnal)

	sts. 1 & 2	a cappella

Conclusion

Although the crossing of borders often happens uneventfully, with little fanfare and interruption, it does make us momentarily ponder the meaning of where we have come from, where we are at the moment, and where it is that we are going. The music we bring to our worship has the potential of being received with kindness and generosity. Making preparations prior to arriving at potentially difficult crossings can greatly increase the possibility of the traveler receiving a desirable welcome. May it always be so. Having planned the trip with care, let us venture out and travel, allowing the Spirit to move among us.

ENDNOTES

1. Kay Kaufman Shelemay, "Crossing Boundaries in Music and Music Scholarship: A Perspective from Ethnomusicology," *The Musical Quarterly*, Spring 1996, vol. 80, no. 1 (Oxford University Press, 1996). Although Kaufman Shelemay focuses on crossing boundaries in music and music scholarship, I believe some of the ideas she presents can be applied to crossing boundaries in worship. I am loosely extracting some kernels of thought from this article to support the image of music as traveler.

2. John 4:23-24.

3. Robert E. Webber, ed. "Seven Styles of Morning Worship," *The Complete Library of Christian Worship*, vol. 3, (Nashville: Star Song Publishing Group, 1993), 111.

4. *Hymnal: A Worship Book* (Elgin, Ill.: Brethren Press; Newton, Kan.: Faith & Life Press; Scottdale, Pa.: Mennonite Publishing House, 1992).

5. Romans 15:5-6.

6. *Hymnal: A Worship Book*, 818, which is based on Psalm 5:1 and *Hymnal: A Worship Book*, 137 "Father, Forgive Our Sins as We Forgive."

7. *Hymnal: A Worship Book*, 143, "Amazing Grace."

8. *Songs & Prayers from Taizé* (Chicago: GIA Publications, Inc., 1991).

9. George Carey, *Spiritual Journey* (London: Mowbray, 1994), 143-145.

10. *Hymnal: A Worship Book*, 101, "Alleluia"; and Psalm 86:1-13.

11. *Hymnal: A Worship Book*, 144.

12. Webber, "Charismatic Worship" by Melicent Huneycutt Vergeer, 117-120.

13. Ibid., 119.

14. Webber, "Seekers' Service/Believers' Worship," 124.

15. Ibid., 126-127.

16. Romans 15:6.

17. All hymns in this festival are from *Hymnal: A Worship Book* unless otherwise noted.

18. John L. Bell, *He Was in the World*, (Glasgow: Wild Goose Publications, 1995) 69.

19. Ibid., 91.

20. Ibid., 87.

Chapter 4

Global Music for the Churches

by Mary K. Oyer

At the end of the twentieth century, we are witnessing dramatic changes in church music. For centuries the organ has been the predominant instrument in the church, both for presenting solo pieces and for leading and accompanying the hymns of the congregation. Its value has been enhanced by the magnificent organ literature from fine composers over five hundred years.

In recent decades, interest in studying organ in music schools has dropped. Pipe organs, for which excellent literature was created, are now being replaced by electronic instruments of various kinds and a broadening of views of what makes an instrument suitable for worship.

The sixties

The 1960s brought an outburst of new styles of hymns, perhaps comparable only to the sixteenth-century Reformation in Europe. The 1560s were especially remarkable: the Lutheran chorale was in full swing; complete Psalters of the Calvinists, English, and Scots were published; and the Anabaptists produced three hymnals, including the *Ausbund*. The impetus for change in the 1960s came no doubt initially because of the Vatican II decision to use vernacular languages in worship, thus replacing the use of Latin throughout the Catholic world. Roman Catholics in Britain and America created hundreds of new songs in English, borrowing frequently from folk and popular styles. At the same time or soon afterward, Protestants produced hymns in styles that called for new kinds of accompaniments. Both piano and guitar gained legitimacy for many congregations, and percussion instruments were a welcome addition in some churches. Contemporary speech in the texts often replaced what had become a special religious language, based on the King James Version of the Bible.

The new styles of hymns were not incorporated immediately into official hymnals; rather, they were grouped in softcover books, like *New Hymns for a New Day,*[1] published as a part of the periodical called *Risk;* the Lutheran *Songs for Today,* 1964; and *Hymns for Now,* 1967.[2] Mennonites published songs of this kind in *With* magazine: *Songs to be Sung, Whistled or Hummed (Right Now),* 1969,[3] and *Festival of the Holy Spirit Song Book*[4] for a special event at Goshen (Ind.) College in 1972. The 1979 *Sing and Rejoice,*[5] coming out of Herald Press in Scottdale, Pennsylvania, represented a compilation of songs of the 1960s and 1970s which seemed to the editor, Orlando Schmidt, to promise lively use for the next decade or so. A number of denominations moved in this direction, providing a softcover complement to their official hymnal.

It is not surprising that global hymns began to appear in hymnals during this exploratory period in history. The Methodists, for example, included nine cross-cultural hymns in their 1964 *The Methodist Hymnal*[6] —one each from Thailand, China, Nigeria, and the Dakota Native Americans, and five African-American spirituals. For *The Mennonite Hymnal*[7] (1969), the committee found six from outside the European-North American world and two African-American spirituals. For Mennonites, the decision to include them was long in coming because of the fear that we might not be able to do them well, perhaps even offending the Christians with whom the hymns originated. The group finally agreed that possibly the texts and tunes would be useful for women's missionary meetings!

Ntsikana's story

When we consider that Westerners had been establishing missions for well over a century, we may find it difficult to understand the hesitation to join in singing with Christians of other cultures. The well-documented story of Ntsikana, a leader of the Xhosa people of South Africa, in David Dargie's "Xhosa Church Music"[8] and Janet Hodgson's *Ntsikana's Great Hymn*[9] may be instructive. A missionary from England had gone to the Xhosa at the end of the 1700s. After years of failure to gain converts, he returned to England. Around 1815, when Ntsikana was attending a wedding dance, a great whirlwind arose and disrupted the party. All that night he and his family stayed awake singing. A vision came to him about a new God whom he should worship, and he created a song in response. He praised a Great Shield; a Thicket (presumably of protection around his house and cattle); a Great Blanket (of both warmth and identity); the Creator of the Pleiades; the Hunter of souls; and the Reconciler of flocks that are fighting. He closed with references to the wounded hands and feet; the blood streaming down for us; asking whether we are worthy of the price and of that promised home.

Looking back from the 1990s, we can easily view this hymn as a remarkable indigenous expression in the language and imagery of the Xhosa people. This is a hymn in its appropriate context, rather than a transposition of the mode of thought of the Western world. When new missionaries came, however, they did not find it satisfactory for worship. Although they had Ntsikana's text in writing as early as 1821, they preferred their own hymns. The new hymns in England at the time were texts like "Holy, Holy,

Holy, Lord God Almighty" and "From Greenland's Icy Mountains." The second of these hymns presented something of the missionary zeal that propelled people to go to a foreign field, but underlying this fervor was the kind of condescension that characterized colonial expressions from time to time:

> *O we, whose souls are lighted*
> *with wisdom from on high,*
> *Can we to those benighted*
> *the lamp of light deny?*

The missionaries undoubtedly found the imagery of Ntsikana's text foreign to their concept of a Christian hymn, but they must certainly have had more difficulty with the music. In England at the time, churches were arranging the melodies of composers like Haydn, Mozart, and Beethoven; melodies from symphonies like Beethoven's HYMN TO JOY,[10] with its lovely arched shapes, which the Western world likes. In contrast, Ntsikana's melody consisted of one phrase that began high and descended to its end an octave lower, as if being pulled down by a magnet. This one melody was used for each line of the text as well as for the brief refrain. The total amount of repetition fit the African oral tradition, but could not have been understood or valued by Westerners. The pitches must have seemed strange to them also. Recent recordings of old people singing the hymn as they learned it by ear make clear that the notes did not have to fall on Western lines and spaces or the white and black keys of a keyboard. A good many sounds were in the cracks between the keys. And they accompanied the songs with hand claps that are difficult for our ears and bodies to assimilate. So Ntsikana's hymn went underground for 150 years, and the culture of the West dominated the Xhosa church. Only now are South African churches of all kinds—Catholic, Protestant, and independent, like the Zionists—valuing this hymn and singing it in many different configurations of voices and instruments.

Cross-cultural hymns

Within the past two decades, hymnal compilers and editors have seen the need for many more cross-cultural hymns. The Methodists published a series of books called Supplemental Worship Resources which included *Songs of Zion*,[11] 1981, a collection of 250 hymns valued by African-American congregations. The editors grouped the songs into sections and described their character: Hymns derived from and shared with the white community, Negro spirituals, and black gospel. They assumed that people who were not raised with African-American singing styles would have difficulty bringing the notes to life, so they presented an introductory section, "Keys to Musical Interpretation, Performance, and Meaningful Worship." Although hearing the music is the best guide for doing it, this written introduction takes away some of the mystery of crossing cultures.

In 1983 the Methodists also published a remarkable book of Asian and Asian American hymns called *Hymns from the Four Winds*.[12] I-to Loh, a Taiwanese ethnomusicologist, edited the collection of 125 works, consisting primarily of indigenous texts and music from Asian countries. The fine editor's Introduction gave helpful general principles for performance to which individual hymns in the book referred.

By the time the Methodists were ready to compile their 1989 *United Methodist Hymnal*,[13] they had developed rich resources on which to draw. They included more than thirty African-American spirituals and gospel songs. Beyond these, there are eighteen hymns from the countries in which Methodists have established missions, many of them Asian.

Mennonites have experienced a similar growth of interest in cross-cultural hymns. Rosemary Wyse and Clarence Hiebert prepared a collection of sixty-three hymns from five continents for the Tenth Mennonite World Conference in Wichita, Kansas, 1978. Subsequent conferences, in 1984,

1990, and 1997, based their written materials for singing on this book. There are a few suggestions for performance; but because the collection was created for a specific event, the World Conference congregations could listen to singers and instrumentalists from around the world to catch ideas for singing the hymns appropriately.

It seemed logical for Mennonites to increase the cross-cultural offerings for the next official hymnal, *Hymnal: A Worship Book*, published with the Church of the Brethren in 1992. African-American songs expanded from two to twenty. The remaining cross-cultural hymns increased from six to forty-three. Suggestions for performance came in the *Hymnal Accompaniment Handbook*[14] in the form of general essays on the music of a continent or a particular area of the world, as well as details for bringing a specific hymn to life.

The response to the inclusion of so many cross-cultural hymns, however, has been mixed among Mennonites. The questions of the 1960s return: Can we sing them "right"? Is it fair to the creators of the hymns to do them poorly?

Other questions emerge which reveal the discomfort with this new type of hymn. For example, what have we had to drop in order to make space for these songs? Whenever a new hymnal appears, most people grieve over the loss of favorite hymns. This is probably especially true for a free church type of worship. Liturgical churches have set prayers and responses, which with years of use move deep into the inner core of being; and they are always present in a service; the unchanging, eternal aspect of the worship. Favorite, often-repeated hymns fulfill this function for Mennonites. Tunes of hymns rather than words alone remain with the elderly as the mind dims. Hymns comfort in dire circumstances. So the loss of the familiar brings serious and legitimate complaints.

Levels of memory

In a book on worship called *Trouble at the Table*,[15] the authors speak about three levels of historical memory.

They acknowledge their indebtedness to a Dutch theologian Edward Schillebeeckx[16] for the basic idea of ordering history in this way. The first level (they call it structural) is long lasting, like the Jewish memory of the exodus and the repetition of naming God's acts in the Psalms. It is at the heart of the belief and rituals of a group. They see it as the center of three concentric circles. The third and outer level (ephemeral) is brief; memory passes quickly. Between the two is the level that participates in aspects of the other two (conjunctural). Some elements pull toward the center of a people's life; others lose their intensity and move to the ephemeral level and may disappear altogether.

If we think of hymns in these terms, the central, structural level for Mennonites today would probably include these hymns in *Hymnal: A Worship Book* (1992): "Holy God, We Praise Thy Name" (121); "I Owe the Lord a Morning Song" (651); "O Have You Not Heard of That Beautiful Stream" (606); "Great Is Thy Faithfulness" (327); and "Praise God from Whom All Blessings Flow" (118). These hymns seem quite entrenched in the church's life and represent the most permanent hymnic values of the group. We mourn their loss when they are removed from our books, though we probably have them in our memory for a time.

The conjunctural level has those hymns that are relatively new but are welcomed wholeheartedly, almost as if we had known them for a long time. For example, in *Hymnal: A Worship Book,* "What Is This Place" (1); and "My Life Flows on in Endless Song" (580) belong here. We cannot be sure that these hymns will join the central, structural level, but they point in that direction, after moving rapidly from newness to a familiar place in worship. We recognize their value to the group when we notice that they are chosen for both weddings and funerals—in both celebrative and grieving situations.

All new hymns enter a congregation's history through the outer circle, the ephemeral level. Here they are tried and judged; and if they light a spark for us, they move inward toward the conjunctural level. On the other hand, they may simply disappear. This level is very necessary to a congregation's life because new songs bring fresh expressions and vital images. But time is needed for testing their value. It is for this reason that a hymnal committee must take a long period of time to make judgments about unfamiliar hymns. The congregations will then continue the process of accepting and weeding out.

Incorporating cross-cultural songs

The sudden influx of ephemeral cross-cultural hymns into *Hymnal: A Worship Book* brought understandable discomfort to many worshipers. Normally a song leader can decipher a Western hymn from the musical notation. But when an Asian or African hymn is notated as if it were Western (most of us could not understand the kinds of notation that exist in their cultures), the songs look overly simple and barren on the page. The notes we see represent only a skeleton of the music, which needs the addition of drums or hand claps or of ornaments and slides in the voice. Often instruments bring the right spirit to the hymn. Although we hear from time to time that music is a universal language which cuts through the usual boundaries separating people, it is far more likely an exclusive language, communicating only with those who are initiated. It must be learned in much the same way a spoken language is learned.

A song leader will naturally feel insecure in leading cross-cultural songs from the page of the hymnal. The best way to learn is to hear the music, preferably sung by a native of the country where the song originated. That is the way music would be learned in many parts of the world where the oral tradition is deeply rooted in the culture. A recording can be helpful, though one misses the movement of the body without the visual.

Another point that troubles many Mennonites is that these hymns appear to be one line only. What will become of the valued four-part singing tradition? *The Mennonite Hymnal* included very few hymns that departed from a four-part setting. For nineteenth-century descendants of Swiss and South German Mennonites, three-part singing had developed in the singing schools which used Joseph Funk's 1832 shape-note book, *Genuine Church Music.*[17] Its name changed to *Harmonia Sacra* in the middle of the century, and the parts expanded to four. These singing schools continued until the middle of our century. Russian Mennonites used numbers, *ziffern,* to help them learn to read music. These educational methods were instrumental in building the fine tradition of four-part singing that *The Mennonite Hymnal* represents. Unfortunately, during the past forty or so years, we have neglected teaching part singing, and the practice is weakening. Eliminating these single-line hymns or adding harmonies to them, however, will not save part singing for Mennonites. Congregations will need to work intentionally to perpetuate and maintain four-part singing.

Considering the difficulty of learning cross-cultural songs, why should a congregation struggle to do it? The Thirteenth Assembly of the Mennonite World Conference meeting in Calcutta, January 6 to 12, 1997, provided an opportunity to examine the values behind the effort. It was an excellent occasion to observe differing approaches to music and to participate in the invigorating experience of crossing cultures with reasonable success and a good deal of pleasure.

Mennonites form a global church, embracing six continents. Music can be an important way through which to learn to know each other because it is one of the keys to understanding a culture. It reveals attitudes toward time and space; toward the body and the realm of the spirit; toward human interrelatedness; and toward learning and passing on traditions.

In Calcutta I had the role of assisting Premenand Bagh, a fine Indian musician, in directing a choir of Indian musicians who were chosen to lead the congregational singing. Choir members came from various geographic locations, languages, and denominations of the Mennonite World Conference. We spent ten days rehearsing, performing, and becoming a choir.

The fifteen choir members and instrumentalists were good musicians. None of them read music, but their oral skills of listening and remembering were excellent. I soon realized that my job was to teach the notated hymns in the songbook by rote; the India Choir in turn sang them for the congregation, most of whom also learned by ear. I quickly developed great respect for the choir's speed of learning and the dependability of their retention. My habit is to focus on the book, with my eyes; in contrast, they caught the song with their ears and knew the music in a way I never will. Oral learning (which in Anabaptist tradition is still carried on by the Old Order Amish and Old Order Mennonites) has a special quality about it, described by an African *griot*, or history singer of Mali, whose duty it was to remember and tell the history of the succession of kings of the medieval Mali Kingdom:

> *Other peoples use writing to record the past, but this invention has killed the faculty of memory among them. They do not feel the past any more, for writing lacks the warmth of the human voice. With them everybody thinks he knows, whereas learning should be a secret. The prophets did not write, and their words have been all the more vivid as a result. What paltry learning is that which is congealed in dumb books!*[18]

The hymns we sang in India from countries with oral traditions tended to be quite different from standard Western hymns. There was a great deal of repetition of both text and musical phrase (a breath span). By comparison, a Western hymn sounds wordy. In Africa one text and musical motif or phrase is repeated many times. A leader may sing a series of phrases with the congregation responding to each with the same refrain-like answer. Indian hymns very often consist of a phrase or two repeated immediately. Those repetitious pieces were so successful for the congregation and such a pleasure to sing in the Indian context that by the last few days of the conference I found myself choosing "Kum Ba Ya" or an African-American spiritual rather than a favorite standard Western hymn. Perhaps repetition is one reason why the songs from the Taizé Community in France lead people so well into deeper levels of worship (see, for example, in *Hymnal: A Worship Book*: "Jesus, Remember Me" (247); or "Veni Sancte Spiritus" (298). The character of a service with much repetition is often less dense and more reflective than a wordy one. A worshiper can be released from a focus on linear thinking and move into another level of worship—a fact that charismatic Christians have known for a long time.

Dance and movement

Dance and movement are closely related to music; Africans find the two inseparable. In some African languages, the same word is used for both dance and music. Mennonites at the World Conference had quite differing ways of relating to the body. The Indonesian church sent a fine choir that presented a choreographed version of a passage from Revelation, carefully controlled. In contrast the Zairian Choir danced through the hymns they sang with such energy that many in the congregation were encouraged to move also; it was an invitation to direct participation, which spilled over into the time following the benediction. Our cultural contexts influence our views of dance. In general the Far Easterners felt more comfortable with no motion or highly stylized, controlled movement. Complex and exciting drumming reached the Indians through the ears rather than the moving body. Africans sense the presence of the Holy Spirit when the entire body is involved. Latin Americans seemed to be close to the Africans' sense of freedom and use of improvisation. North Americans and

Europeans were somewhere in between.

Views of space and time

At the Calcutta world conference, the acoustics of the lovely large tent, or *shamiana,* favored sight rather than sound. The space was open, not enclosed and resonating. There were no walls to reflect sound back into the congregation, so the people's sound moved outward, and street noises and prayer calls came in to the group. It was strikingly different from the ideal of the Western world. Christopher Small[19] believes that Western culture makes a spatial frame around its music: "We place the sounds in a building or other space built or set aside for the purpose and carefully insulated to keep the sounds of everyday life from entering—and also perhaps to keep the sounds from escaping into the world—while the performers are placed on a platform, apart from the audience." It took some time to adjust to the difficulty in hearing the singing of the large group. Eventually I found the openness of space refreshing and attractive.

Just as the Western world prefers a spatial frame or enclosure for its music, so it values a temporal frame—an enclosure in time. We expect silence before we begin a piece of music and immediately after the sound ends. A precise beginning and ending are possible within this frame of silence. Not all groups of people, however, view precision in time as a high priority. For the Latin American caucus of around thirty people who led the congregation in worship one morning, how to begin the singing was an uncomfortable question. They asked for a signal for the first note or two and then moved through each song with ease and vitality. I suspect that in a less formal setting, they would not have worried about a precise beginning but would have entered the song when it felt natural to do so. African hymns often began with a solo voice. The responding congregation then had no difficulty knowing when to enter or how fast to sing.

These spatial and temporal frames point to a characteristic of the Western arts that deserves attention, especially because it seems to hold little importance for many people of the world. Why do some cultures prefer to isolate works of art from the flow of life—choosing to enclose performances of sound and to frame and thus isolate a song with silence? Has it something to do with control rather than letting go freely?

In the fourth century B.C., Aristotle described the time art of drama as comparable to the unity of the human organism. As it flows through time, he said, it has a noticeable beginning, middle, and end; we can always know where we are. In addition, it is organized around a climactic moment of complexity from which the work diminishes to a logical ending. Western music, as well as drama, tends to be organized this way. We have learned the signals, and unconsciously we have the comforting knowledge of where we are. Perhaps a deadline-oriented society needs this kind of security.

Time in the non-Western world has a different effect. The music seems to this listener to have greater uniformity and little urgency to conclude. Much music in sub-Saharan Africa, for example, moves in a kind of cyclical pattern with an infinite variety of detail. It has no fixed or prescribed ending, reaching its conclusion in its own good time and leaving the same piece different in length each time it is performed. Justus Ogembo, a Kenyan friend,[20] described the difference in views of time between Africa and the West with the analogy of eschatology. Christian missionaries, he said, broke into the African view of time, which consisted of a strong present and past, with a message of looking forward to a future, toward the end of time when God would come and bring justice to humanity. The thought patterns and even the grammar of some ethnic groups could not accommodate the concept of a future, especially of a distant future. The music of the two cultures reflects and symbolizes differing views of time and of moving toward the future.

Such observations can be useful for understanding and identifying with brothers and sisters from other parts of the world. By observing how they make music and what seems to be important to them, we receive insights into aspects of their lives beyond music. And the openness to try to understand can help us to see ourselves more clearly: What are we saying about our view of the cosmos, beyond the words and the music, when we sing?

The theme of the India world conference came from Revelation 3:22, "Hear What the Spirit Is Saying to the Churches." The Indian Mennonite bishop Shant Kunjam composed a theme song on that text. Not only did he create the song; he reached across cultures and wrote it down in Western pitches and rhythmic notation. Its Indian form is quite unlike that of a Western hymn. Each line is repeated before going on to the next. The repetitive ending sounded as if the song was moving out into the world beyond our *shamiana*.

The several kinds of drums and shakers the Indian Choir used were basic to the energy of the song; therefore, the written form (Exhibit 1, page 81) is simply a skeleton to supply a few directives. In addition to drums, we heard the distinctive sound of a harmonium—a short keyboard played with one hand and accordion-like bellows operated by the other. The player of an electronic keyboard brought improvisatory elements to the whole.

We sang the song in the three dominant languages of the conference: Hindi, Telagu, and English. We returned to it so frequently that it served as a genuine theme song. We did hear the usual favorite "Praise God from Whom All Blessings Flow" from the Indonesians, and we sang it vigorously in the congregation. This time, however, the people went away with "Hear What the Spirit Is Saying to the Churches" in their ears.

Conclusion

It is possible that the era of complete domination of non-Western cultures by the Western world is passing. Ntsikana's hymn has won in southern Africa and extends to hymn books in the Far East. Bishop Kunjam's hymn won the hearts and minds of Mennonites from five continents and symbolizes hope in a healthy cross-cultural interchange.

Exhibit 1

Hear What the Spirit Is Saying to the Churches

Written for Mennonite World Conference, Calcutta, India, 1997. Used by permission of Bishop Shaut Kunjam.

ENDNOTES

1. Geneva: World Council of Churches, 1966.

2. *Songs for Today* (Minneapolis: The American Lutheran Church, 1963); and *Hymns for Now* (Chicago: Walther League, 1967).

3. Scottdale, Pa.: Herald Press, 1969.

4. Goshen: Goshen College, 1972.

5. Kitchener, Ont., and Scottdale: Herald Press, 1979.

6. Austin C. Lovelace and Carlton R. Young, *The Methodist Hymnal* (Nashville: Abingdon Press, 1964).

7. Scottdale: Herald Press; and Newton, Kan.: Faith & Life Press, 1969.

8. Mary Collins, et al., eds., *Music and the Experience of God*, (Edinburgh: T. & T. Clark, c. 1989), 62-69.

9. Cape Town, 1980.

10. *Hymnal: A Worship Book* (Elgin, Ill.: Brethren Press; Newton : Faith & Life Press; Scottdale, Pa.: Mennonite Publishing House, 1992), 71.

11. J. Jefferson Cleveland and Verolga Nix, eds., *Songs of Zion* (Nashville: Abingdon Press, 1981).

12. Nashville: Abingdon Press, 1982.

13. Nashville: United Methodist Publishing House, 1989.

14. Elgin: Brethren Press; Newton: Faith & Life Press; Scottdale: Mennonite Publishing House, 1993).

15. Thomas Troeger and Carol Doran, *Trouble at the Table* (Nashville: Abingdon Press, 1992), 119-121.

16. *Jesus: An Experiment in Christology* (New York: Seabury Press, 1979), 576-577.

17. Winchester, Va., 1832.

18. D. T. Niane, *Sundiata: An Epic of Old Mali* (London: Longman, 1965), 41.

19. *Music, Society, Education* (London: John Calder, 1980), 25.

20. In lectures given at the Goethe Institute in Nairobi, Kenya, December 3, 1987.

Chapter 5

Contemporary Church Music Issues

by Christine Longhurst

"I just don't know why they had to go and change the way we sing at church," the elderly man complained. "I don't know half of the songs we sing. We don't sing in harmony anymore. And we sing so fast—I can't keep up. Why can't we sing like we used to?"

This elderly man's experience is not unique. Many people find themselves adjusting to changes in contemporary worship music. Attitudes and practices concerning the role of the congregation in music making, the way singing is led, how worship music is chosen, the texts we sing, even the role of the choir are being evaluated, altered, or discarded altogether. The changes are affecting congregations in different ways, but all are affected by changes in the way music is used in worship.

Changes in worship music related to our changing understanding of worship

The shifts in worship music haven't simply been change for the sake of change, although to some it may appear that way. Rather, the motivation for change is directly related to changing attitudes about community worship. Worship music has also been impacted by pivotal shifts in thinking about the nature of God. In his study on trends in recent American hymn texts, Samuel Rogal states:

> Corporate worship moved away from an atmosphere pre-
> dominated by a fear and awe of a God who would inflict
> punishment for even the slightest disobedience. Following
> World War I, particularly, American sacred song moved
> toward a love of and a gratitude toward God. Worship
> became both individual and comfortable.[1]

This emphasis on the role of the individual in congregational worship is central to the changes we are experiencing. Popular books such as Anne Ortlund's *Up with
Worship*,[2] Robert Webber's *Worship Is a Verb*,[3] Barry Liesch's
People in the Presence of God,[4] and many others have encouraged us to see worship, not only as service to God, but also
as actual encounter with God. They describe worship as a
relational activity, where worshipers come to dialogue with
God, to find wholeness and healing. They clearly point to
the responsibility of individuals in the worship setting.

Don McMinn, in his article "Preparing the Heart for
Worship," suggests that

> God is not just seeking worship. He's seeking worshipers
> (John 4). Otherwise we could just insert a compact disc of
> praise music, put it on continuous play, and be done with
> it. God would be appeased and we could do our own thing.
> But it's not that simple. God is looking for worshipers—
> people.[5]

This shift in thinking from *worship as the service offered to
God by a community* toward *worship as dialogue between God
and an individual* has radically reshaped our expectations of
worship. Whereas our worship traditionally tended to
focus on the intellectual (the sermon seen as the most
important single event of the worship hour), today we see
significant movement toward more balanced worship.
Worshipers today want to involve all the sources of human
response—mind, body, and emotions. Many congregations

are exploring the use of visual stimuli (images and symbols) as they work with light, banners, and colors. Churches are also experiencing greater freedom in physical expressions of worship, whether that be through clapping, the raising of hands, the use of the tambourine, or the exploration of traditional forms of liturgical dance. The move toward increased emotional involvement has been even more obvious and has had its most significant impact on our worship music. The emphasis on the individual experience of worship has also affected leadership styles and the ways in which services are crafted.

The impetus for change comes from a desire to more fully experience God in worship. People are hungry for worship that has an impact on their lives. As *Beyond* magazine's Flora Stormer suggests,

> *Spiritually speaking, unless practical benefits or potential applications are immediately evident, I classify the experience as a waste of time. I want to be efficient above all else. In a sermon, tell me something that's relevant to my life now. Let's sing like it matters. Let's make every moment poignant and profound. . . . Let's see my life become more Christ-like before my very eyes.*[6]

While many elements make up a worship service, music is seen by most people as one of the most significant. As well, because of the prominent role it plays, music is often noticed more than other aspects of the service. For this reason, we need to give special attention to how changing ideas about the nature and purpose of worship affect music.

The congregation's role in music making

Mennonite congregations have traditionally been integrally involved in worship music. Hymn singing has been central to worship; people learned to sing four-part harmony as children in church. The singing of hymns was augmented by traditional performance groups: choirs, ensembles, and instrumentalists.

At first glance, the role of the congregation in worship music today appears to be as integral as it was in the past. In fact, congregational singing—expressing praise, adoration, confession, and thanksgiving to God—is one of the focal points of contemporary worship. The growing emphasis on congregational song has coincided, in many churches, with a deliberate move away from traditional performance groups (choirs and ensembles).

A closer look, however, reveals a more complex picture. While the emphasis on congregational singing remains high, some styles of song appear to be losing a congregational focus. This is equally true for both praise and worship music and contemporary classical forms. Take, for example, "Come, Let Us Sing"[7] by Brent Chambers; and "Lions and Oxen"[8] by Carol Doran, ISAIAH'S DREAM tune. (Exhibit 1, excerpts, page 101)

The rhythmic complexities of the Chambers piece make it difficult to perform, even for a well-rehearsed group. The word-painting chromatic structure of Doran's melody and accompaniment is equally inaccessible to large groups of people. This is not because congregations are necessarily musically illiterate. History suggests, however, that unrehearsed groups of people singing together naturally tend to simplify complicated rhythmic and melodic music. Historical examples are plentiful. Martin Luther's "Ein Feste Burg" ("A Mighty Fortress Is Our God") is a good example. The original in *Hymnal: A Worship Book* (329)[9] is not unlike much of the syncopated contemporary music used today. The version that has come down to us, however, is almost unrecognizable in comparison. The same trend exists in many contemporary choruses. The version of Mark Altrogge's "I Stand in Awe," which appears in *Worship Together* (63),[10] is significantly simpler than the original composition. Complex congregational music rarely remains unchanged over time. In the meantime, the relative success of complex musical styles, whether traditional or contemporary, often depends on the expertise of the music leadership.

It is interesting to note that many contemporary hymnals are making use of traditional folk songs. These simple, yet beautiful, traditional melodies include tunes such as BUNESSAN, THE ASH GROVE, and O WALY WALY, KINGSFOLD.

The success of GIA Publication's hymnal, *Gather*,[11] (which contains songs such as "Healer of Our Ev'ry Ill," "Shepherd Me, O God," "On Eagle's Wings," "Here I Am, Lord") is in part due to the singable, folk-like quality of the music. The same is true for the appeal of the music of the Iona Community in Scotland.

The role of the individual in music making

It would seem logical to suggest that, given the present shift toward a more personal style of worship, the singing of individuals in contemporary worship should assume primary importance. But the assumption that everyone can and should sing in worship is being challenged on a number of levels.

It is not at all uncommon to hear individuals say, "I don't sing." One of the factors here is a change in what is seen to be the ideal vocal sound. For most people, the ideal sound is one that is supported by some form of sound amplification, including some amount of reverberation to add warmth and depth—the type of sound most of us only make naturally when we're in the shower. It is no wonder that, with that ideal sound in our heads, many of us shy away from the sound of our natural voices.

The acoustics in our churches also play an important role in discouraging individuals from singing. Despite what we read and hear about the importance of the congregation in worship, many contemporary church buildings are built more like concert halls than anything else. This results in a natural dampening of the sound that emanates from the congregation and an amplification of the sound that comes from the platform. Congregational singing in many churches is hard work.

Overly enthusiastic leading or accompanying of the music can also discourage congregational singing. High volume levels coming from the front of the sanctuary (whether from organs, worship teams, or instrumentalists) can easily send the message that individual voices are not really important or that they are not good enough on their own.

Sensitivity, toward "seekers," and a growing awareness that our congregations are not as homogeneous as they once were are challenging our assumptions about traditional four-part harmony. With many people from outside the Mennonite tradition joining Mennonite churches, a skill that was once assumed can no longer be assumed. Hymnals published in the past decade clearly show a trend to lower musical settings based on the assumption that all voice parts will likely be singing the melody.

The role of music leadership

Leadership styles are also experiencing a dramatic change in order to accommodate new ideas about worship and the role of the congregation. In many cases, individual leadership is being replaced by group leadership (worship teams) or no visible leadership at all. The criteria used to choose music leadership is as much spiritual as it is musical. In fact, contemporary music leaders are often called worship leaders in recognition of the fact that their role goes beyond simply leading the singing.

There is a feeling in contemporary worship that leadership should be unobtrusive—that is, that it should not interfere with the dialogue taking place between individuals and God. If there is to be commentary, it should be of the kind that leads people more deeply into that dialogue.

Carol Doran and Thomas Troeger, in their fascinating book *Trouble at the Table*,[12] present an interesting theory regarding effective worship leadership. Central to their theory is an analysis of two different states of being that people experience: intra-dependence and extra-dependence.[13] Intra-dependence is "the state of depending on ourselves. Most adults have to be intra-dependent most of their lives. . . .We pour out energy to take care of ourselves and others."[14] Constant intra-dependence can be exhausting. This theory suggests that all human beings need times when they can step back from the demands of intra-dependence.

> *We periodically need to change out of that role; we need to receive instead of give, to surrender control instead of take control, to become, in a word, "extra-dependent," to depend upon another. The church at work invites people to become dependent upon the only One who is ultimately dependable: God. When worship "works," people find themselves renewed by the experience of extra-dependence so that they can return to their daily lives and take responsibility for using the gifts that God has given them.*[15]

According to this view, it is important for humans to move back and forth between these two different states of being. They suggest, however, that the leadership and structure of worship services can often keep worshipers from experiencing extra-dependence.

> *Intrusive instructions from the leaders interrupt this process by keeping everything tightly controlled so that the service never leads us into a state of extra-dependence upon God. The result is eventually a feeling of boredom because worship becomes just one more intra-dependent activity in which we cease to expect an encounter with God. We go through the motions but our heart is not in it.*[16]

Amateur or professional?

The move toward music leadership that is both spiritual and musical has resulted in some confusion among musicians. On the one hand, the signals are clear: leaders do not need to be professional musicians in order to lead worship music. The signals to those who are professional musicians are far less clear, and many find it difficult to find their own place in contemporary worship. I recall a recent conversation with a talented musician in my congregation. When I asked her if she would be willing to use her gifts in our worship, she indicated some uncertainty about how her gifts would be received. "The music I would bring is quite different from what we usually have," she suggested. "I don't know if I would fit."

There are various ways in which our worship music can become exclusive. We've often excluded people based on the amount of talent or training they have. We also have a long history of excluding those instruments deemed unsuitable for worship (among them, at different points in history, the organ and the piano). Many styles of contemporary worship now use nonclassical instrumentation, such as guitars, synthesizers, and drums. While it is good to see these instruments gradually find their place in worship, it would be a shame if they did so at the expense of those instruments currently deemed to be less popular. In the same way, worship music leaders and worship teams (whether trained musicians or not) need to be careful not to simply become a new elite. During the past few years, I have had regular conversations with a musician from a charismatic congregation here in Winnipeg. Years ago this congregation led the way in contemporary worship team leadership, and their success was duplicated by many other congregations. Of late, a growing sense of frustration has developed within the congregation, primarily because many musicians in the congregation can find no outlet for their musical expression. Those in the two select worship teams have become the new elite.

Music's role in bringing emotion to contemporary worship

The shift toward worship that attempts to balance the intellectual, emotional, and physical responses has had a tremendous influence on contemporary worship music. This is not the first time in history where such a shift has taken place. The overwhelming popularity of gospel song in the late nineteenth and early twentieth centuries was due, in no small part, to a desire for increased emotional expression. Many parallels could be drawn between traditional gospel song music and the contemporary musical expressions we encounter today. In fact, some congregations are experiencing a resurgence of popular old gospel songs. The new Mennonite Brethren hymnal, *Worship Together,* includes such old favorites as "Victory in Jesus" and "Wonderful Grace of Jesus," which had been excluded from the previous hymnal.

I have been intrigued to see some of my students discover "I Stand Amazed in the Presence of Jesus, the Nazarene" and similar traditional gospel songs. Set to contemporary rhythm and accompaniment, they appear very similar to the praise and worship choruses with which many are familiar.

This desire for increased emotional expression has led to some significant changes, both in the music being sung and how it is chosen and used in worship. Among the many changes are the following.

More time and less text in singing

Many congregations have recognized that eliciting a genuine emotional response can take time. One result is to have extended periods of singing within the worship service. The singing in these congregations can easily fill a half-hour block or more. Even congregations with a more traditional approach to worship music are tending toward longer periods of singing.

At the same time, the amount of text used in extended

singing packages has decreased significantly. As well, texts are often repeated a number of times. Those individuals who continue to feel most comfortable with intellectual worship often find it difficult to understand why a single stanza is repeated four, five, or six times.

"This is an intentional moving from a logical-intellectual mode of perception to one of meditation and spiritual understanding," suggests Melicent Huneycutt Vergeer. "The call 'Let all that is within me bless God's holy name' is extended to harmonize left and right brain!"[17]

It is intriguing to note that the emergence of these shorter worship songs happened almost simultaneously in various parts of the world. Examples are: the Scripture in Song Movement, which originated in New Zealand; the Vineyard Movement; and the Praise and Worship Movement. The Taizé Community in France (which has brought us such pieces as "Jesus, Remember Me," "Veni Sancte Spiritus," and "Bless the Lord") may use a somewhat different musical language, but their philosophy ("music as prayer") is the same.

Engaging melody, intimate texts, and rhythm

It is no secret that one of the simplest ways to impact human beings musically is by using strong rhythm. Our physical response is immediate: We clap our hands, tap our toes, stamp our feet, or snap our fingers. Emotional response is also immediate. It takes a great deal more energy and effort for music to affect people intellectually. Much contemporary music utilizes engaging rhythm and emotional melody to reach listeners physically and emotionally.

The language of our worship music has become increasingly intimate, with phrases such as "You Are Beautiful Beyond Description," "Abba, Father, Let Me Be

Yours, and Yours Alone," "Come, Holy Breath, to Seek and Know Me," "O Lord, You're Beautiful." Much contemporary worship music seeks to address God directly, rather than simply speaking about the attributes of God.

Choosing music for worship

The organization of the tables of contents of hymnals published in the 1960s and 1970s give clear indications that hymns and songs were chosen topically. Most often, choices were made to match specific sermon topics or Scripture passages.

Increasingly, the need for hymns and songs to match a specific topic has become less important in contemporary worship. A look at the tables of contents of some more recent hymnals shows that function is the preferred method of organization. The placement of hymns and songs within these hymnals reflects the order of activities within the worship service: gathering, praising, confessing and forgiving, affirming, thanking, etc. Music is chosen to enhance our experiences in worship; to walk with us through the drama of worship; to provide us with words in our dialogue with God. This shift from topical to functional criteria helps explain why songs like "I Will Enter His Gates" continue to receive such high usage in so many churches.

In addition to functional criteria for music choices, there is a strong movement toward experiential criteria; that is, songs are chosen to lead people into an experience of the presence of God. The Vineyard Movement (which has had a significant influence on many churches) has developed a system of categorizing choruses, ordering them in a specific sequence for worship. The Five-Phase Worship Order[18] (outlined by John Wimber and Eddie Espinosa) consists of the following phases: **invitation**— "the lyrics should address the people and call their attention to worship"; **engagement**—"the people draw near to God"; **exaltation**—"the people sing out with power"; **ado-**

ration—"the dynamics may gradually subside and melody may have a smaller range"; **intimacy**—"is the quietest and most personal."

Another popular pattern for choosing music experientially is the fourfold pattern based on the tabernacle. This pattern takes the worshiper through the gates of the tabernacle, into the outer court, through to the inner court, and ends in the holy of holies. "There is a narrative quality to the movement as the worshipers travel through distinct moods and stages of spiritual intensity through the use of music."[19]

In addition to functional and experiential approaches to music selection, we must add musical, that is, choosing musical pieces based primarily on the characteristics of the music itself (key, meter). With the growing popularity of extended packages of music sung in worship, the selection of songs according to their relationship to each other has assumed greater importance. It is interesting to note that numerous songbooks and hymnals have seen fit to add a "keys and meters of songs" index.

Disposable music and the ongoing search for new material

The contemporary church music scene is characterized by an endless search for new material and a corresponding disregard for music that has become obsolete. Contrary to popular opinion, the disposable music phenomenon did not originate in the last half of this century; it has been a natural part of worship music renewal for centuries. A look at the work of past songwriters illustrates this. Charles Wesley wrote a total of 8,989 hymns and poems over his entire lifetime; few contemporary hymnals contain more than twenty of his works. The popular gospel songwriter Fanny Crosby wrote approximately 8,500 songs; most hymnals contain fewer than ten. Despite the historical precedents, reaction to the concept of disposable music continues to be quite mixed. In one Winnipeg church, some members actually sat on their books of supplemental music when asked to sing from them. On the other side of the spectrum are those who express antipathy for all bound music, as if it is not of the Spirit.

Whatever the response, the move toward more experiential and emotional worship music guarantees that the turnover rate of worship songs will continue to be high. The nature of much of this music is testimonial, focusing on the personal experience of the writer. In addition, many songs are both written and composed by the same individual (a trend we also saw in turn-of-the-century gospel music). It only stands to reason that many of these expressions of worship will wear thin over time and will need to be replaced.

Many churches have identified a strong need for this type of ongoing colloquial expression. It is impossible to identify in advance which of these songs will stand the test of time and become classics in their own right. Who could have guessed that Peter Scholtes' "They'll Know We Are Christians by Our Love"[20] (1966) would last so long or experience a recent upsurge in popularity?

The downside to the high turnover of worship songs continues to be the congregation's finite level of tolerance for new material. Some contemporary music styles are providing us with more successful approaches to new music. Among these are the use of recurring congregational refrains; the creative use of ensembles, worship teams, and song leaders to teach the congregation; the growing popularity of easily singable folk styles; and the relaxing attitudes toward the pairing up of new texts with familiar melodies.

Observations on music styles

We are living in an exciting time. All around us are creative new music resources. From the tremendous upsurge in contemporary hymnody (Brian Wren, Ruth Duck, Shirley Erena Murray, Thomas Troeger, and others) to the refreshing folk music of the Iona Community; from the responsive music of the Roman Catholics to the praise and worship music of the Vineyard Movement; and the international music of the world community, we are surrounded by a rich variety of musical style and emphases. Many congregations are finding that one single music resource is too limiting and are finding alternate ways to access supplemental material (the use of overhead transparencies; add-on binders or folders in the pews; additional songs included in the worship order as needed; and the purchase of published supplemental material). The rise of comprehensive copyright licenses has made many of these approaches more accessible than before.

Despite the wealth of new and old resources, however, some congregations continue to use only a fraction of what is available. There are many possible reasons for this. Some congregations may be unaware of the wide variety of music available or may not know how to access it legally. Others may be in environments where comfort levels with diverse musical languages are limited. Many of us have experienced the difficulty of working a variety of musical styles into one service. Or congregations may have purchased comprehensive music resources that may tend to limit their vision ("We've just bought the new hymnal. What more do we need?" or "We've just purchased this all-inclusive chorus book/overhead collection. This will last us for a while!"). Another factor may be copyright licenses which restrict us to certain groups of publishers. (The only way to have ongoing access to the exciting new material from the Roman Catholics is to purchase a separate copyright license.)

It is encouraging to see movement away from the "hymns versus choruses" debates of the 1970s and 1980s. Even more encouraging is to see the boundaries between musical styles begin to blur as different genres of worship music begin to overlap stylistically. In many cases, it has become almost impossible to clearly categorize music style.

For example, is Graham Kendrick's "Shine, Jesus, Shine" a hymn or a chorus?

Observations on the texts we sing

Even as varying styles of contemporary worship music appear to be moving closer together, approaches to text seem to be moving further apart.

There appear to be at least two different approaches to text in contemporary worship music. One approach places significant emphasis on text: the crafting of words and the exploration of imagery and ideas. Contemporary hymnody would be one clear example of this type of approach. Musical environments, while important, seek to serve and augment the text.

The other approach appears to be primarily music-driven. In this kind of worship music, the music itself assumes an importance equal to, or even greater than, that of the text. Texts tend to be relatively brief and often repetitive; the use of texts from Scripture and biblical imagery is common. General categories of this type of music would be the music of the Taizé Community ("Jesus, Remember Me") and much of the praise and worship genre.

Just as music-driven worship music has brought much freshness and balance to contemporary worship, the varying styles of text-driven worship music are bringing insight and creativity to traditional expressions of worship and are continuing to challenge believers to deeper spiritual growth and understanding.

Contemporary language, imagery, and issues

Twentieth-century hymnody appears to be leading the way in the use of inclusive language. Already in 1978, with the publication of the *Lutheran Book of Worship*,[21] we saw efforts to begin to revise the language used to refer to people (e.g., brotherhood, mankind, etc.). Almost all major hymnals since that time have struggled with the issue of inclusive language, and many have expanded the issue to include the language we use for God. (Can God only be viewed in male images such as King, Shepherd, and Master?)

Concern for inclusive language has not only been limited to revision work, however. Individual hymn writers have been exploring new language and imagery for God and have written exciting new hymns which explore the experiences and perspectives of all people: young and old, male and female.

Although there are differences of opinion, many text writers believe strongly that traditional hymns can find new life in contemporary worship if some of the archaic language expressions are updated (words such as "shouldst," "dost," "wilt," and "doeth"). Some of the most successful revision work appears in the *Psalter Hymnal*[22] (edited by Emily Brink) and in *Hymns for Today's Church*,[23] produced by the Jubilate Hymns team.

The Bible continues to be a primary source for metaphor and imagery in contemporary church music; however, contemporary hymn writers are enriching the traditional images with twentieth-century perspectives and experiences. The difficult issues of death, illness, divorce, doubt, anger, abuse, etc., all find expression in the work of modern hymn writers.

The changing relationship between text and music

It is fascinating to trace the relationship between text and music over the past century or so. In earlier times, songs were given musical environments as needed, and a text might well be set to a variety of different common tunes. With the publication of several popular hymnals in the latter part of the nineteenth century, many hymns came to be "married" to specific tunes. The influence of the gospel song movement of the nineteenth and early twentieth centuries helped solidify the idea of text and tune marriages. Most of the twentieth century has seen this relatively strict relationship between text and tune.

Recently, however, the field of hymnody is beginning to see a breakdown in this way of thinking and congregations are gradually regaining the freedom to use familiar musical environments for a variety of different texts, old and new. Some contemporary hymn writers (Jane Parker Huber, Ruth Duck) have chosen to write primarily for familiar tunes.

The same freedom does not seem to apply to contemporary praise and worship music, just as it likely never will for most traditional gospel songs. Many of these songs are personal expressions, often written and composed by one individual. Their inspiration is often as much musical as it is textual. Even so, it is worth exploring some of these new melodies to see whether or not they can provide interesting new environments for contemporary or traditional texts. For example, in *Worship Together,* Margaret Clarkson's text "We Gather Here to Bid Farewell" is set to Twila Paris' tune LAMB OF GOD (453); or Charles Wesley's traditional "Oh, for a Thousand Tongues" is set to Merla Watson's WATSON (106).

Presentation of text

Given contemporary hymnody's strong emphasis on text, it has always seemed somewhat ironic that the presentation of those texts (interlined between lines of music in a hymnal) seems to draw more attention to the music than to the words. The presentation of these texts in publications put out by individual hymn or song writers is much friendlier and often includes two settings of the words: one interlined with the music and one written in poem form. Recent hymnals are becoming somewhat more creative with the appearance of text, occasionally printing texts in poem form with a suggested tune noted underneath.

It also seems ironic that the use of overhead projectors

for song texts (which, although sacrificing some musical elements, do succeed in giving worshipers a better appreciation for text) are used overwhelmingly for contemporary music which is more music-driven than text-driven.

A vision for the future

What about the future? Experience indicates that change will continue to be with us. Things that are new today will be replaced by something else. Things that are old may come back. But as God's people continue to search for meaningful ways to worship together, one thing will not change: there will be no easy or pat answers when it comes to questions of how to worship God. As Marva J. Dawn suggests in *Reaching Out Without Dumbing Down: A Theology of Worship for the Turn-of-the-Century Culture:*[24]

> *We dare not make worship too easy, for God is always beyond our grasp. Worship cannot be only cerebral or only emotional, for God is mysterious and wise. Worship must be unceasingly comforting so that through it God will address our suffering. It must be perpetually paradoxical so that we know we must worship forever.*

Exhibit 1
Excerpts

Come Let Us Sing

Brent Chambers

tol Him with mu - sic and song. For the Lord our Lord __ is the
kneel be - fore God, our great king. For He is our God, __ and

great __ God, __ the great King a - bove all __ God's
we are His people, __ that's why we shout and __ sing.

Lions and Oxen Will Feed in the Hay
(tune: Isaiah's Dream)

Carol Doran

Thomas H. Troeger

Carol Doran

Blood will not dark - en the earth that God made.
Ripe for the judg - ment the Lord will or - dain. Lit-tle child whose bed is
Filled with the knowl-edge and love of the Lord!

Text: Thomas H. Troeger (born 1945). Music: Carol Doran (born 1936). From *New Hymns For the Life of the Church* ©1989 Oxford University Press, Inc. Used by permission.

ENDNOTES

1. "Some Trends in Recent American Hymn Texts," in *The Hymn,* vol. 48, no. 1 (January 1997), 30.
2. Ventura: Regal Books, 1975.
3. Nashville: Star Song Publishing Group, 1992.
4. Grand Rapids, Mich.: Zondervan Publishing House, 1988.
5. *The Church Musician,* vol. 48, no. 3 (Spring 1997), 11.
6. Editorial in *Beyond* (Winter, 1, 1997), 3.
7. Brent Chambers, "Come, Let Us Sing," *Scripture in Song,* 1985.
8. Carol Doran, "Lions and Oxen Will Feed in the Hay," tune ISAIAH'S DREAM, Oxford University Press, 1989.
9. Elgin, Ill.: Brethren Press, 1992.
10. Winnipeg, Man.: The Christian Press, 1995.
11. Chicago: GIA Publications, Inc., 1994.
12. Nashville: Abingdon Press, 1992.
13. The authors credit the work of the Grubb Institute in Great Britain for this concept.
14. Carol Doran and Thomas Troeger, *Trouble at the Table* (Nashville: Abingdon Press, 1992), 101.
15. Ibid., 101.
16. Ibid., 102.
17. "Charismatic Worship," in Robert Webber, ed., *The Complete Library of Christian Worship,* vol. 3 (Nashville: Star Song Publishing Group, 1993), 120.
18. Barry Liesch, "The Style of Contemporary Worship," in Robert Webber, ed., *The Complete Library of Christian Worship,* vol. 3, 212.
19. Ibid., 212.
20. "They'll Know We Are Christians," F.E.L. Publications, 1966, assigned to Lorenz Corp., 1991, Dayton, Ohio.
21. Minneapolis: Augsburg Publishing House, 1978.
22. Grand Rapids, Mich.: CRC Publications, 1987.
23. Carol Stream, Ill.: Hope Publishing Company, 1987.
24. Grand Rapids, Mich.: William B. Eerdmans Publishing Company, 1995, 289.

Chapter 6

Congregational Singing as a Pastor Sees It

by Gary Harder

I write this chapter as our congregation is on the verge of moving into our new facilities. For ten years we have discussed, debated, explored, argued, researched, fought, reasoned, voted, and re-voted our way toward this moment.

"It has to be multifunctional," some said. "We've got to be able to use our building every day of the week to justify the million dollars. And that means getting rid of the pews and having movable chairs."

"But we insist it has to be a worship space first of all," others said, "with the look and the symbols that draw us to God. We don't want just any old gymnasium look. Better keep the pews."

"We've got to be practical though," others argued, "and design a serviceable building that will accommodate all our needs. With land costs as they are in Toronto, we have to use every inch of space available."

"We shouldn't go it alone," was heard loudly and clearly. "We have an exciting opportunity to partner with another ethnic group, perhaps with our Spanish brothers and sisters."

"I think it should be 'simple' in truly Mennonite tradition," others theologized, "so that we remove our class consciousness and make both our rich and poor neighbors feel welcome."

"And what about acoustics?" cried many loud voices. "Good congregational singing is so central to our worship life that acoustics have to be a primary concern." Some folks told horror stories of how badly many new Mennonite facilities they had visited worked acoustically. "All the music has to be amplified. Absolutely dreadful." One voice was even heard to mutter, "When you push a microphone in the face of everyone who sings, you not only change the music style of the church, you change its theology."

And so it came to pass that "acoustics" became a significant theme in our new design. Our worship space even underwent a modest redesign after acoustical engineers had had their say (though we don't fully trust them. "Do they have any idea about 'Mennonite' singing?"). Our old building "sang very well." We take pride in our strong and vibrant congregational singing. We are aware that singing is close to the heart of our spirituality, our soul. Our interim worship space at St. Clair O'Connor (our Mennonite intergenerational housing community), while offering a wonderful connection with many of our seniors, was absolutely dead acoustically. We struggled to retain any joy in our singing.

On Christmas Eve we move into our new "meeting room." Our ears are on full alert. We have planned a "lessons and carols" style of Christmas Eve service. We will know immediately "whether it will work for singing."

Societal context

We hear much these days about premodernism, modernism, and postmodernism. "We are living in postmodern times," say the analysts of social culture. Like it or not, worship life is being dramatically affected and altered by the winds of postmodernism.

"There is an increase in the search for a deeper spirituality," say the analysts, "but a decrease in expressing this spirituality in the organized church. Unless our worship styles change dramatically, the organized church will become totally irrelevant to the spiritual search of our younger generation."

"Our Western world is dominated by a consumerism mentality" observe some, "and so we are tempted to buy into religious consumerism too. People, especially seekers are viewed as a market, consuming objects that have to be entertained. Music especially is seen as a commercial tool, part of an entertainment package catering to people's (younger people's) likes and acculturated tastes." The buzzwords are "seeker sensitive" and "visitor friendly."

"I'm not a Mennonite. I can't sing like that," said a visitor to our church. "I love the sound of the harmony. I'm in awe. But I feel totally left out. Can't you sing at least one song each Sunday that has only the melody so that I can follow along and hear what I should be singing?"

"But do we have to totally sell out to our culture in order to be relevant?" argue others. "We shouldn't have to enlist the popular music of a consumer culture in order to attract a younger audience today. Aren't Christians (especially Mennonite Christians) supposed to be counter-culture rather than slaves to culture? Besides, the 'throw up' music today is musically boring and theologically simplistic."

"Many young people today are growing up musically sophisticated," observe some. "They are highly trained and enormously talented. And they are fully at home with diversity. Let's finally move beyond the fruitless 'chorus versus hymn' dichotomy and embrace a variety of music styles."

"Nah, I don't buy into that 'return to an acoustical sound' you young adults are talking about," said a high schooler. "Give me a highly amplified beat any day. But do

I want that in church? Nah, I think church should be different and special."

Our social context is a postmodern one. What do we embrace? What do we challenge?

Personal context

I bring a huge personal bias into the discussion of music in worship. My musical tastes were shaped by a family that loved classical music. I grew up with Bach, Handel, Mozart, and Brahms. Even as a teenager, I thumbed my nose at pop music. As a teen I wanted to emulate my father who was a farmer and the church choir conductor. I went to Canadian Mennonite Bible College to study music so that I could go back home to Rosemary, Alberta, to farm and conduct the church choir.

Our family home breathed music. Mom played the piano. Dad conducted the church choir and often led the hymn singing. When the congregation sang poorly, Dad would sometimes stop the hymn and reprimand the congregation: "Wir schleppen ja" (we're dragging), or "das schneidet so sehr" (it's 'cutting,' or out of tune). This introvert of few public words would publicly say that if we are singing to the glory of God, then we had better put our best effort into it and sing as if we wanted to give glory to God. And he would re-start the hymn and the congregation would sing with new enthusiasm.

We four sons all took piano lessons. It was unthinkable that we wouldn't learn to play music and to sing. Luxuries there were almost none in our house (no indoor toilet or running water). But from the time that we had electricity, there was a record player of some sort out of which flowed the music of the masters.

Strangely, we seldom sang together as a family—all the music around us and all this musical ability, but we seldom sang together. But then it's hard to make your family sound like a choir when you've got one alto and five bass-baritones. Probably the real issue though was perfectionism in music. If you can't make it sound as good as the Robert Shaw Chorale, don't do it at all. We missed something important by not singing together more: pure enjoyment, a closeness, and a nonverbal worshiping together as a family.

On Dad's deathbed thirty-three years ago, when none of us introverts could think of anything more to say and yet we felt we hadn't quite said good-bye in the way we wanted, we decided to sing for Dad. And so we put voice to "So lang mein Jesus lebt," "Lieber Vater hoch im Himmel," and "So lange Jesus bleibt der Herr." We knew them by memory. Tears came. It was an intimate moment, a good good-bye.

I was twenty-two years old when my father died. Our family turned to music to help us in our grieving. We immersed ourselves in the texts and music of *A German Requiem* by Brahms, a favorite of Dad's. Such is the nature of our family music tradition.

My undergraduate degree in college is in music. Conducting was my love. I had an enormous struggle, not resolved until after my first year in seminary, trying to choose between pursuing a career in music or in pastoral ministry. My struggle resolved itself intuitively and even mysteriously the summer following a wonderful month-long immersion in a music seminar sponsored by the two Mennonite colleges in Winnipeg. Seemingly satisfied and happy, my heart could hear more clearly God's gentle but clear call to pastoral ministry. I have never had regrets or second thoughts. The thing was resolved. Music would be a secondary love, but a love it has remained.

I was the choir conductor in two of the churches I pastored. Apart from the simple joy of making music, leading the choir always made me face firsthand the issue of fitting music integrally into the worship service. The music the choir sang could not be only "performance" or "entertainment" ("thank you, choir, for that number"). If the choir didn't contribute to the theme or liturgical development or emotional tone of the worship service as a whole, it couldn't be sustained with integrity. The struggle within me was the recognition that as a choir conductor I needed a month or two lead time to prepare music for a given Sunday morning, while as a preacher I often scrambled from one week to the next to find a text, a theme, and a sermon. The preacher within me often couldn't give the conductor within me enough time to do justice to integrating the music fully into the worship service.

Music also continues to play a very significant part in my spiritual nurture and in my spiritual preparation to preach or to lead worship. An unfailing Sunday morning ritual at our house, a rut at least twenty-five years deep, is to listen to the music of J. S. Bach. I listen to Bach, meditate, and go over my sermon. The music of Bach grounds me, gives me a spiritual center. Without it my spirit feels somehow weaker, not fully prepared for the spiritual energy required to lead others in worship.

These then are some of my personal biases. Musically, I got stuck some two centuries ago, feel most at home in the classical tradition, and prefer a natural to an amplified sound. But the pastor's musical tastes (or lack thereof) and preferences are not an adequate basis for choosing the musical repertoire of the church. Professionally, I think that music needs to be fully integrated into the worship service as a whole. Theologically, I believe that worship is not a performance but a participatory act of encountering God.

Is there any hope then of saying anything significant or even interesting about music and worship in a consumer-oriented postmodern world?

The participatory nature of public worship

Anabaptists have stressed that worship involves the whole community. The gathered people are not an audience of individuals gathered to be fed or entertained by leaders set apart. Worship gains its Spirit-led power when the people as a whole enter the presence of God, led there to be sure, but coming as a participatory community (Col. 3:12-17; 1 Cor. 14:26). This would suggest to me that when it comes to music in worship, the most important music in the church is congregational singing. As much as I enjoy and am often led to encountering God by a good choir, an instrumental ensemble or solo, or a well played piano or organ, these, in my mind, are not the center of a church's music ministry; congregational singing is. This means to me that participation and vitality are key factors.

Our congregations are, for the most part, intergenerational. All ages, from children to the aged, need to find their voice and their identity reflected in what they sing. All ages need to be encouraged to fully express and/or develop their musical gifts. Most congregations, especially urban ones, are increasingly cosmopolitan and cross-cultural. This fact would already make a case for enlarging our musical expression and style to include hymns from other cultures (*International Songbook*[1] and *Hymnal: A Worship Book*[2] do a great service here) and to include some unison singing for those who are not used to reading parts. We can only be enriched by including the global church in our hymnody. And hopefully we can be fully "gender inclusive" in our singing. Inclusive language has been and still is divisive in some of our congregations. I would plead for sensitivity here but for a sensitivity that moves clearly in the direction of inclusivity.

Vitality and energy and creativity are key here. Sameness and tameness kills the spirit. The problem that many young people have with traditional hymns is not the music itself, nor, for the most part, the text, but the lethargic way these are often sung. Congregational singing needs a power, an "aliveness," regardless of which musical style is chosen. (Worship leaders and preachers, regardless of their musicianship or singing ability, are so visible that the congregation often takes its emotional cue from them and reflects their enthusiasm, or lack thereof, in its own singing.)

Congregational singing is, I think, a barometer of the spiritual vitality of the church. It is an indicator of how deeply faith is experienced. Energy and animation and full participation are more important than choral purity. If congregational singing is central, then we have to put our best musical efforts here, whether it is in selecting appropriate hymns, leading them well, or training the whole congregation to sing as well as possible. For me this means encouraging even the "musically challenged" to sing out and to love singing. Let even the monotones praise the Lord in full voice. But training the whole congregation should also include teaching children and young people how to sing in harmony and teaching them the joy of singing.

At some levels we in the Mennonite church are probably still somewhat suspicious of professional musicians in the church. We are afraid they will be elitist or too esoteric for us, or they will intimidate us amateurs. But we urgently need both their leadership in our worship and their gifts in leading and training the whole congregation musically. My experience is that many of them share their gifts gladly. They teach, help, model, mentor, and encourage.

Hospitality and inviting outsiders into our home

As a family or as a congregation, we have an identity, an atmosphere (culture), a set of house rules, and certain comfortable ways of doing things. Musically, each congregation has an identity, including a hymnody, which reaches to the core of its being. But if it is hospitable, it will take into consideration the hymnody of the outsider it is inviting in. This doesn't mean that the congregation changes its own identity to cater to the stranger. It does mean, however, that it is sensitive to the experience of the stranger. Over a period of time, the newcomers will join with the old-timers to gradually forge a new identity and a more inclusive hymnody.

When we invite persons from other cultures into our

homes, we gladly serve them particular Mennonite foods (though not exclusively, especially if there are repeat visits), just as we enjoy being served their specialties in their homes. We enrich each other's culinary experience. With hymnody the problem comes, not from having an identity, but from being too narrow and exclusive in our musical diet. For example, it seems to me that the "choral versus chorus" battle is a loser all around. We have visited many unhappy choices and dichotomies on our people, whether that be choral versus chorus; music that is "seeker sensitive" or for regulars; music for youth over against music for the gray hairs; amplified versus acoustical sound; traditional versus new; harmony versus unison; and music for the mind and heart or music for the whole body (especially the feet).

In the words of one of my sons (another closet musician who is professionally involved in church ministries other than music—yes, the sins of the fathers are visited on the next generation), "The dichotomy between 'hymns' and 'choruses' is limiting and unhelpful. It reduces the vast musical and textual richness and variety of both centuries of musical development and hymn writing and of the many different contemporary musical expressions to only two categories. There is quality and legitimacy within each of these many styles, just as there are poorer examples of each. Healthy vibrant worship integrates a diversity and variety of musical styles and expressions, even though congregations may lean in certain directions."[3]

I find it significant that young people and young adults are often far more eclectic in their musical tastes than my generation is and can enjoy a much greater diversity in styles than I can. They move easily from Bach to jazz to pop to chorus. So let's not get them stuck on either only hymns or only choruses. There are rich resources from various styles and traditions. Many of our children are growing up with far greater musical sophistication and skill than my generation had. Many of them are enormously talented and trained. Let's challenge them to use all of their musical powers in the service of our Lord. If we do, the boundaries around "hymns" or "choruses" will never be able to contain them.

In choosing music we do need to take into account the history and present context of our churches. There are important traditions and memories and faith expressions that give meaning to a group. We can't abandon these, but we can push out the edges. We can become more inclusive. We can broaden our congregational repertoire. We do need to be hospitable to the stranger. For me personally, and for our congregation, I think, the core hymnody remains the more traditional hymn style enriched and broadened by an amazing variety of wonderful new music resources. I am so pleased with many of the new hymn **texts** in *Hymnal: A Worship Book*.[4] I am glad to be able to turn to the new texts to find themes and poetry to connect with my preaching.

Much more can still be done to develop and incorporate good, solid contemporary hymns into our worship. We can encourage the poets and composers among us to unleash their creativity here. We can try to incorporate the best of the new hymns in our worship; hymns that speak relevantly to our context; are integrated, wholistic, thoughtful; and offer wonderful visions of what God is doing in our world.

Longing for wholeness and for integration

We want to love God with all our heart and mind and soul and strength. We want to combine belief and experience and action in our faith. We resist compartmentalizations that separate and segment our faith or our worship into small boxes. When it comes to worship, my orientation is to insist that music must be at the service of worship as a whole. It needs to be integrated into the larger theme or liturgical structure or spiritual/emotional tone of the whole.

I chose my doctor of ministries dissertation (*Touched by*

Transcendence: Shaping Worship That Bridges Life and Faith) on the basis of a rather disturbing experience. It occurred at a Mennonite music seminar. Two hundred and seventy musicians from across Canada, Mennonite Brethren and General Conference Mennonites, gathered in Winnipeg in February 1985, to sing Brahms and Bach under the baton of Robert Shaw. The week was a musical, emotional, and spiritual mountain top for me. But I was dismayed with the answers to a very innocent and unpremeditated question I asked some twenty to twenty-five of these Mennonite music leaders during several lunchtime conversations in groups of six or seven around a table:

"How do you coordinate your music ministry with the overall worship ministry of your church? How do you work at integrating music with the worship theme of the morning?" To my dismay, they all said they didn't. Without exception, the people I asked said they did their own thing (chose music they happened to like), and the minister did his own thing (none of them had women ministers at that time). They never got together to plan or coordinate their ministries. The music leaders, of course, all laid the blame for the lack of consultation on the minister. "He doesn't know anything about music anyway." Or "He chooses his theme the last part of the week and that doesn't give us enough lead time." Or "He's not interested in our suggestions." The point was that in the churches represented by these music leaders, there was no planning that included the major worship participants. The music was a separate island disconnected from any meaningful integration with whatever else happened in worship. The result then is that the order of worship is not dignified by a coordinating theme, and the various components of the service become a collection of more or less interesting and/or worshipful pieces. The bulletin has become a program and the worship leader a master of ceremonies.

In the Toronto United Mennonite Church, we are trying to find new ways to plan worship that is more integrated.

Most recently we are both excited and frustrated by a worship-planning format we are trying. Our preaching team (four lay members of the congregation plus me as pastor) explores themes and texts, and, of course, schedules preachers. One member of the worship committee then acts as a coordinator and gathers all the major worship participants for a given service one week in advance during our coffee hour (preacher, worship leader, song leader, accompanist, and children's storyteller). The preacher gives the text and a short explanation of the theme. Then everybody brainstorms around these. It's amazing how creative this process sometimes is and how integrated the worship services sometimes are. But the process often breaks down, sometimes because we preachers don't have our act together early enough, but more often because one or more than one of us is away on any given Sunday and just not available. Yet when we meet, the results are very satisfying.

It is immensely satisfying when music contributes to a particular moment in worship. Perhaps what is needed at a given moment is a Taizé short piece, or a Bach choral, or a guitar-led chorus or folk hymn, or a song from Guatemala or Africa, or a chant, or an African-American spiritual, or a gospel song, or a Brian Wren or Bradley Lehman contemporary hymn. A team can cast the net widely and help make the music serve the rest of the worship. I long for such wholeness.

Transforming our world, not being conformed to it

Chapter 12 in Romans, with its challenge to "not be conformed to this world" (Rom 12:2), has always had a significant place in the Mennonite canon. My interpretation today is that we need to be responsive to our culture but not controlled by it. Some of the old dualisms of the clear separation between church and world or of "Christ against culture" are surely unhelpful.

When it comes to music, we can't help but notice that our children and young people are being profoundly shaped by the pop (rock) culture of our day. But does it mean that we bring this music into the church wholesale so that we will keep our young people? Do we really need to cater to the popular music of our commercial and consumerist culture in order to survive? Is there a way of being "in the world" but not fully "of the world" that has integrity **and that has worship appeal**? Can we engage the culture without becoming the culture?

My reading of young people is that they are often bored with traditional hymnody. But neither do they want, as an alternative, that the church fully embrace pop culture. They may choose that as their music to listen to at home. But they know it is commercial, meant to entertain, and often espouses values incompatible with their faith. They do not want to take it wholesale into church. They do want some recognition that some of the sounds and rhythms of contemporary culture are now a part of who they are. But they also want the church to be different, to reflect Christ more than the culture. They want energy and life and a beat, but they also want depth.

Perhaps we always need to be in the process of creating a new culture in the church. We always need to be in the process of naming our experience and transforming our culture in the light of Christ. We bring with us a tradition, in the best sense of that word, but continually create a new vision, a new reality. That is why we urgently need new hymns that express the reality of our experience and our faith in some of the musical idioms which can bridge the older world and the newer world.

Depth in worship that fully embraces mystery, joy, and pain

"What is the nature of great music? What is the nature of good worship? What are the attributes and states of being, that allow it to happen? For me its absolute minimum conditions are a sense of mystery and an admission of pain.["5] In these words, Robert Shaw, musician, is striving for depth. Life is the most whole when we acknowledge a deep sense of mystery—in great music, in good worship, in life itself.

There must be a deep sense of mystery in worship. We come before a God whom we cannot control or manipulate or even fully understand. Of course, God is revealed in Scripture, in Jesus Christ, and in our experience. Even so we see only "in a mirror, dimly" (1 Cor 13:12). We await a time when we will see God face-to-face. In the meantime we acknowledge mystery. In the meantime we struggle with perplexing life situations, with unanswerable questions, with the unfathomable reality that God does indeed work in mysterious ways. Our worship will have depth if we open ourselves to the mysterious God.

Worship is also a place to bring our pain. Each of us comes to a worship service with a whole backlog of feelings and experiences, joy and pain mixed, hopes and fears struggling with each other. We all carry some hurt—some strained relationships; some physical, emotional, or spiritual unwellness; some anxieties or fears or worries; some unfulfilled hopes or plans or expectations; some sin or guilt; or grief over one kind of loss or another; or questions about life or about death or about faith. To live is to experience pain. In worship we are able to bring our pain to a healing God in the context of a healing community.

If we are in touch with mystery and with pain, then joy and celebration will come naturally and even spontaneously. But if we attempt to develop an isolated praise and celebration culture disconnected from pain and mystery, it will in the end be shallow and hollow. Surely we need more joy and more praise and more celebration of God's love and power in our worship. But we don't want just froth. Mystery and pain and joy are all experiences of depth. Music in worship must reflect that depth. I do not think that depth equals complexity. Sometimes a very simple melody or a very simple text can be very profound. But there is much very shallow music out there (both musically and theologically). Little ditties and little pieties won't reach through to the core of our being.

The Psalms are a model to me of bringing together mystery and pain and joy at a very deep level. They embrace all of human experience, the lovely and the unlovely, and dare bring it before God. They even dare bring God before God in accusation. In worship we long for depth. We long for a place where mystery and pain and joy are all recognized, all experienced fully. I think we want our worship music to help take us there.

Conclusion

Our congregation had its first service in our new facility on Christmas Eve. We chose a "lessons and carols" kind of service so that we had every opportunity to sing together. A flute broke the candle-lit silence with the melody of "O Come, O Come, Immanuel." The congregation ventured the unison opening lines, held its collective breath, and then plunged into the harmony chord "rejoice." The sanctuary filled with an awesome sound. Smiles broke out all over the place. The acoustics were wonderful. We sang with smiles, with joy, with some tears, with power, with love for our Savior. The place works acoustically. Now it's up to us to continue to create a music ministry that fully utilizes this worship space for the full glory of God.

ENDNOTES

1. Doreen Helen Klassen, ed., *International Songbook* (Carol Stream, Ill.: Mennonite World Conference, 1990).

2. *Hymnal: A Worship Book* (Elgin, Ill.: Brethren Press; Newton, Kan: Faith & Life Press; Scottdale, Pa.: Mennonite Publishing House, 1992).

3. Mark Harder, notes from a workshop, March 1, 1997, St. Jacobs, Ontario.

4. *Hymnal: A Worship Book.*

5. Robert Shaw, "Worship and the Arts," sermon preached February 1, 1985, Winnipeg, Manitoba.

Chapter 7

Anticipating God-Presence: Recovering a Primary Essential for Worship

by George D. Wiebe

Four people, among them prospective contributors to this volume, were enjoying a lively conversation over lunch at a local restaurant. Subject: worship and music in worship. A former missionary to Colombia and Bible professor decided to play the devil's advocate (in this case, God's!). With the abruptness of a talk show interviewer, he halted the rambling conversation, turned to one of the members, and asked point-blank, "When you think of worship and music, what's your passion?"

Stunned silence! The interesting, convivial atmosphere had suddenly changed into some heart-wrenching searching. Do I have a passion about some aspects of worship and music to which I have devoted a major part of my life?

"Strong conviction and deep concern" would possibly better describe my interest in the topic of this chapter. There are two personal factors that have contributed to this interest.

First, my training and experiences as a musician (choral conductor) have brought me into contact with some extraordinary musicians whose work was characterized by a wonderful, infectious sense of anticipation for exquisite music making. Music under their direction always had a strong sense of "eventfulness"—of continuing, unfolding, musical, and spiritual revelations. I became increasingly fascinated with the possibility of structuring entire worship services (including worship-oriented sacred concerts) in which the sequence of music and other items would communicate a recognizable design and a sense of purposeful forward motion. For that flow and a sense of constant anticipation and arrival to happen, it was necessary that, not only ALL the musical and spoken elements be well prepared, but also that the focus and design of the service be communicated to the singers and other participants.

Second, I had the opportunity to observe and experience services of worship characterized by rapt expectation for the Spirit of God to speak with precision and relevance to the needs of the worshipers. These happened in smaller house church gatherings that we were a part of in the 1970s and early 1980s, as well as in very large gatherings like the one held in 1972 at Notre Dame University in South Bend, Indiana. In those early years of the fresh outpouring (movement) of the Holy Spirit in all major and minor denominations in the world, such gatherings for praise and worship were wonderfully alive. So often I was left wondering, "Why isn't there more of this joyful anticipation and lively hope in the churches that purport to have answers as to how the Holy Spirit should blow? Why not let the Spirit, who gives birth to joyful hope and expectation blow as it chooses?"

This chapter has been organized around two foci. The first part will focus on the relevance, the biblical foundations, and the positive possibilities of expectant worship based on a lively Christian hope. The second part will present the exercise of anticipation in the preparation and enactment of corporate worship, with particular reference to musical ministry.

A lively Christian hope

The word HOPE, which is popularly relegated to mere wistful desire, is used here in the biblical sense as awaiting and trusting in the ongoing activity of the Holy Spirit in the world and in the resurrected life with Christ beyond our physical death. This ultimate Christian hope will be referred to as the "long-range hope," illustrated by a continuous horizontal line.

Long-Range Hope

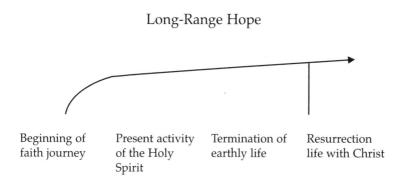

| Beginning of faith journey | Present activity of the Holy Spirit | Termination of earthly life | Resurrection life with Christ |

The terms **Expectation** and **Anticipation** will be used interchangeably to convey the idea of waiting and looking forward to God's prospective enabling and blessing within the short-term periods of preparing and doing worship. These short-term expectations can be graphically symbolized by the small arcs. The downward pointing arrows signify the constant incitement and supply of anticipation of God-presence and divine help for these times of preparation and worship.

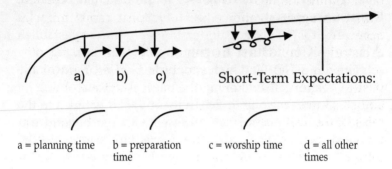

Long-Range Hope

a) b) c)

Short-Term Expectations:

a = planning time   b = preparation time   c = worship time   d = all other times

Relevance of topic

According to one dictionary, hope is the "cherishing of a desire with expectation of fulfillment or obtainment." Hope in this sense is the dominant life force by which we live, move, and have our being. Animals live entirely in the present. When they "anticipate the future," they do not experience it as future.[1] Human beings, on the contrary, concentrate all their interest in the future. It is not natural for humans to live only for today.[2] We are created by God to apprehend and realize life-enhancing goals and values, e.g., the development of gifts and abilities for the common good, both now and for the future. Hope enables us to passionately believe that this is possible. Hope is, tersely stated, "the stuff of life" without which "life is not worth living."

The Bible is preeminently a message of eternal hope. It is a record of petition and response; of waiting and receiving; of search and discovery; and of promise and fulfillment. Inherent in all of these antithetical statements is a period of waiting out the possible and the "not-yet-realized." That tension can lead to a state of anxiety or "be changed into joyful and faithful expectation leading to fulfillment," i.e., from hoping and believing to seeing.[3]

In much of our preaching and teaching of the Bible in

Mennonite (and other) churches, the deeds of God have been confined almost exclusively to the past. God **created;** Christ **brought** salvation; the Holy Spirit **came;** miracles **occurred.** It is, of course, understandable that we establish a historical foundation by thoroughly familiarizing ourselves with **what** God did and **how** God worked in the past—Creation, deliverance of Israel, and the coming of Christ. However, in focusing on what God did, have we missed the essence of the message of a sovereign God whose very nature is to "ceaselessly create unheard of things?"[4] Since the Bible consistently witnesses to: (1) a God whose central nature or character remains unchanged (i.e., consistent, faithful to God's self); and (2) a God whose nature is to create astonishing new things, then it follows that this God can act as astonishingly today, and in the future, as in biblical times.

Such considerations have captured the passionate interest of some of our foremost twentieth-century German theologians like Johannes Metz, Juergen Moltmann, and Wohlfahrt Pannenburg. The Theology of Hope Movement, which these theologians launched, began in the mid- to late sixties and continues to hold the interest, not only of the theological world, but also the world at large. The movement had two sources of inspiration: (1) the scholarly interest in eschatology or the biblical teaching about the future which has preoccupied religious thinkers (and lay leaders) for centuries; and (2) the considerable interest in the future generally—for planning and projecting in industry, communications, education, human ethics, leisure, and the arts.[5] Undoubtedly, the anticipation of entering the third millennium has greatly heightened this interest. Futurology, as a science and as a vocational discipline has become, not only respectable, but also a much sought-after area of expertise in the forecasting of and planning for the various human endeavors which make up civilization.[6]

According to the theologians of hope, Christian faith had to be redirected from being past or present oriented

(Christ alive here and now), to being future oriented. In other words, Christians should live in an eschatological model. Moltmann states this well:

> *From first to last, and not merely in the epilogue, Christianity is eschatology, is hope, forward-looking and forward-moving, and therefore also revolutionizing and transforming the present. The eschatological is not one element of Christianity, but is the medium of Christian faith as such, the key in which everything in it is set, the glow that suffuses everything there in the dawn of an expected new day.*[7]

For Moltmann, it is more important to see Christ as the "coming one" than as the "historical one" (as in the writings of Albert Schweitzer, for example) or as the "here and now one."[8] Thus, life in the present, according to both Moltmann and Metz, is not defined by a God who is behind or above us, but by the God who is continually **before** us! Although the shortcomings and pitfalls of an exclusive "God-before-us" stance are immediately apparent when considered with what the Bible promises about God's immanent presence,[9] the futuristic shift represented by this theological movement was, and still is, a most timely one. A theology of hope can serve both as a corrective and as an incentive for a lively faith par excellence for those who have become stuck in God's work in the past. These astute theologians have provided parameters that can guard against much of the popular, sensational teaching and forecasting of God's and our future!

A lively long-range hope in Christ's continuing revelation of himself (to be fully realized and experienced after our entry into God's presence upon completion of our earthly life) opens new doors for Christian living and for worship. The unprecedented, rapid growth of pentecostal, charismatic, and evangelical denominations in the third world countries can only be explained by the strong hope in eternal life, as well as in the expectation that the God of the Bible who created signs and wonders in the past continues to create similar "unheard of things" now and will do so in the future.

The worship services of these fast-growing fellowships are characterized by uninhibited, enthusiastic praise; rapt anticipation; and an atmosphere of infectious love. The gifts of speaking in tongues, prophecy, healing and deliverance, commonly regarded as the distinguishing features of pentecostal churches, are welcomed but are not the reason for or focus of the service. Rather, they contribute to the strengthening of the body of believers and the stirring of latent talents in music, dance, drama, teaching, and preaching. Harvey Cox, in his recent book, *Fire from Heaven*, gives a fascinating account of how the love and compassion, which God's spirit awakened within a new Brazilian pentecostal fellowship, is beginning to result in productive programs on behalf of the poor and underprivileged.[10] We do indeed have much to learn from this.

In his book, *The Church in the Power of the Spirit,* Juergen Moltmann vividly describes an ideal model of life and worship in the power of the Spirit.[11] Christ is worshiped as the crucified yet risen Lord, who is transformed into divine beauty as the Lord of glory. The new life under his lordship is to be celebrated as the "feast without end, as joy in existence, and as the ecstasy of bliss."[12] The spirit of the risen Christ is what should make our lives a continual festival. Easter should be the feast of freedom celebrated by the "laughter of the redeemed, the dance of the liberated."[13] It is to be, in the words of an Easter hymn by Paul Gerhard, "ein rechtes Freudenspiel" (a true game of joy).[14]

There is much here that validates and dignifies the kind of God-presence and holy joy experienced in the pentecostal church, which Harvey Cox observed in Brazil.[15] Both Moltmann and Cox are pointing toward the same jubilant worship. Moltmann is describing what **could** and **should** happen, and Cox is giving an eyewitness account of what **is** happening. Any serious thinking and personal involvement of those responsible for preparing and leading worship cannot dismiss the powerful potential of a lively, long-term hope to inspire, inform, and energize our worship services. With that in mind, we move to group worship.

Corporate worship: anticipation of God

This section is addressed to those who plan, preach, and lead in worship, with particular reference to the work of the minister of music. Second, it also has something to say to worshipers most directly engaged in these responsibilities.

"Be still, and know that I am God!" (Psalm 46:10).

Planning for worship should begin with stillness. Most creative ventures are preceded by a period of silence, during which the composer, artist, or writer is open to new images or ideas. We think of Beethoven and Brahms on their habitual walks through woods and meadows, gathering inspiration for new themes and musical ideas that became the material for some of the greatest symphonies ever composed.

Dietrich Bonhoeffer,[16] in the introductory statement to his book *Who Is and Was Jesus Christ?* begins with a stunning statement: "Teaching about Christ begins in silence." This is not, he warns, a mystical silence, but the ultimate reverence before Christ, the inexpressible WORD.

It is in the silencing and quieting of our own spirits that we recognize the need for the fresh wind of the Holy Spirit to renew and illuminate our minds before we engage in the planning for worship. Because of the familiarity of the biblical materials and because the words of the hymns we sing are familiar, we are always in danger of failing to acknowledge the vitality and sovereignty of the Spirit's power which defies all domestication. Karl Barth,[17] in his delightful little volume *Evangelical Theology,* has a brilliant and inspiring chapter on "The Spirit." Although it is addressed in particular to theologians, it has equal validity for pastors and anyone responsible for working with Scripture, and in this case, with the words of hymns and other sung music for worship. The words that Barth wrote in 1962 are as relevant and powerful now as they were then:

> *He, the Holy One, the Lord, the Giver of Life, waits and waits to be received anew by theology as by the community.*

Then, toward the end of the chapter, Barth addresses himself, not only to theologians, but also to every Christian:

> *The Holy Spirit is the vital power that bestows free mercy on theology and on theologians just as on the community and on every single Christian. Both of these remain utterly in need of him. Only the Holy Spirit himself can help a theology that is or has become enduringly conscious and aware of the misery of its arbitrary devices of controlling him. Only where the Spirit is sighed, cried, and prayed for does he become present and newly active. Veni creator Spiritus! Come, O come, thou Spirit of life!*[18]

He concludes the chapter with a verse from Paul's letter to the Corinthians: "The Spirit searches all things, yes, the deep things of God" (1 Cor. 2:10).

Those powerful words remind us of the story of Jacob wrestling with an angel. There are times, when confronted with the awesome task of preparing for and leading in worship, where we too, like Jacob, need to pray with dogged perseverance and relentless expectation: "I will not let you go, unless you bless me." Then we read about God's response to Jacob's prayer. "You have striven with God and with humans and have prevailed" (Gen. 32:28b). "There he blessed him" (Gen. 32:29).

Our concern with carefully, logically structured worship services, significant as they are, can never replace the prerequisite of crying for God's help and blessing for ourselves and for our task. Therein lies the hope for a lively

God-presence as we plan and prepare the service of worship.

But now follows the very practical question: How might one begin to plan a service in a mode (not to be confused with mood) of expectation? Perhaps a typical scenario drawn from personal experience could illustrate some principles and approaches.

It is 10:00 a.m. Tuesday morning. I am sitting at my desk in the church where I serve as minister of music. Before me are some open Bibles and a blank piece of paper. I have just met with the two ministers and the secretary to review the week's activities. Some time was devoted to an evaluation of last Sunday's service. We have also had our morning coffee and our share of friendly banter. The mood is quite upbeat.

I have also attempted—before I arrived at the church— to still my restless spirit. I prayed and sighed for the Spirit to become present and newly active in my life and in the lives of my family and co-workers. Now I must exercise anticipation and a will to freshly reengage in the work of planning another service.

It is a privilege to do this work. I am grateful for the enthusiasm and commitment of the staff and the singers I work with. I am also thankful for health, energy, and enthusiasm for the task. I do indeed look forward, and the Spirit is helping, enabling!

I read the Scripture lessons for the upcoming service— sometimes in three languages: English, German, and a halting Russian. (Would that I knew Greek!) I try to single out the focal message of the passage while taking note of what else is being implied in the text. My regard for the preaching task of the pastors is burgeoning: "Lord, bless them as **they** are preparing." Meanwhile, titles of hymns, choral responses, and recently rehearsed anthems are presenting themselves, inspired by the reading of the Scriptures.

But now I need help. I go to the pastor next door. Here is a treasured opportunity for the exchange of ideas and insights on the Scripture passage. I also submit my first choices of hymn selections. Together we evaluate the theme, content, and singability of the music. The exchange of ideas extends to other aspects of the service, such as developing the children's feature from the Scripture lesson and sermon focus as a prelude to the sermon or interpolating a choral response like "O Lord, Hear My Prayer" (*Hymnal: A Worship Book,* 348) to reinforce and personalize the pastoral prayer.

I go back to my desk charged with new insights and with anticipation for a service that should go well! Hymn and anthem choices are finalized and placed in proper sequence. The writing of a paragraph or two for the bulletin, entitled "Hymn-bits," which provides biographical background or hymnic comments on one of the hymns in the service, virtually completes the paper preparation for me, but one thing remains. I go to the other minister who will be leading the service and provide him with a rough draft of what I have done. I share with him my sense of the design and flow of the service.

Four hours later, at 2:00 p.m., I submit copies of the draft of the service to the secretary and the two other ministers. There still may be a few minor changes tomorrow, but otherwise, the paperwork is complete. By now, my inner ear is buzzing with the melodies and harmonies of the music to be rehearsed on Thursday, and my mind is anticipating ideas about how the musical selections might be rehearsed. This Tuesday's planning time, begun in a spirit of expectation, has concluded with added anticipation of the study and rehearsal of the music selected, but heart, mind, and ears are also beginning to anticipate what could transpire at the worship service on Sunday, still five days ahead!

Anticipation of God-presence in practice

A well-planned service on paper, if not prayerfully and carefully envisioned, worked through, and rehearsed with the potential audience in mind, will remain just that—a service on paper. It must, like the notes in music, "come off the page." We focus now on creating anticipation in practice.

Scenario: It is Thursday, 7:00 p.m. The members of a highly accomplished praise and worship band have just arrived for their weekly practice for a fast-paced, carefully choreographed, praise and worship service which meets regularly on Sundays in the city of Winnipeg. The leader, Gina, a bright, vivacious young keyboard lead, sets the mood and the pace. All the other musicians have developed expertise on their instruments: percussion, bass guitar, regular guitar, and violin. There are also three vocalists to provide background for the congregational singing and two vocal soloists.

Gina comes well prepared. For weeks before she has worked closely with a worship planning team. Together they have caught a sense of the Spirit's leading for this particular service. She is thoroughly familiar with all aspects of the service, the Scripture passage and sermon title, the gist and point of the little drama that is to be done. She has selected the music for every segment of the service, plus some extra for subsequent Sundays. She has worked out all the vocals and instrumentals and discussed choreography and lighting. (Yes, this church uses strobe lights). The group knows Gina is ready. They also know that this could be a hard night's work.

The band huddles to pray for specific guidance for themselves, the pastor, the drama group, and any other participants. The anticipation of another evening of intense, exacting rehearsal is keen. The practice begins.

At 9:00 they break for coffee and sandwiches and review what they've achieved so far and what still needs to be done. Gina hints that it may take another hour and a half before everything is right. It does! At 11:00 p.m. they huddle again, giving thanks for what has been accomplished and asking for God's presence and help for Sunday. They keenly sense that they are responsible under God to capture the ears, hearts, and minds of hundreds of people, predominantly young people, some of whom have heard very little about the gospel.

We need not be surprised with a pastor and a drama group, both equally equipped and dedicated, that there are two services each Sunday to seat all the people. People have been scurrying to the worship center—eager anticipation written all over their faces.

By this time some readers may be muttering under their breath, "This is not our kind of music. It doesn't belong in church. This band is doing this for its own glory—jeans, leather jackets, boots, strobe lights, overhead screen, and all—just promoting itself for the next compact disc. And all that holy huddling for prayer—do they think they are holier than the rest of us? And so little concern for congregational singing, let alone four-part singing."

Such responses are understandable, particularly from older people or younger classical music enthusiasts. The changes in music and worship style have come too fast for many.

The purpose of this chapter is not to evaluate the kind of music and style of ministry represented by this band. The chapter on contemporary music can give us some criteria and handles for that. However, there are several significant aspects for a vital music ministry exemplified by this praise band that apply to even the most traditional church choir:

- a deep conviction that the Spirit can work in and through us to reach people;

- a teamwork approach to long-range advance planning;

- discovery of greater unity and freedom through intentional (not merely pious) prayer for each other and continually renewed visions for ministry;

- more zeal for perfecting the music so the choir members are freed to let the music and message get "off the page" and into the hearts of the listeners.

A revitalization of these basics in any musical group and its leaders cannot but greatly heighten enthusiastic anticipation of worship. The implementation of these basics is left to the vision, courage, and resourcefulness of all those involved in leadership.

Anticipation of God-presence in the worship service

"I was glad when they said to me, 'Let us go to the house of the Lord!'" (Psalm 122:1).

The final section will reflect on the anticipation of God-presence before and during the service.

Giving   Anticipating

Scene 1:   A Sunday morning worship service of a Mennonite Umsiedler church, in Bielefeld, Germany.

It is half an hour before the service. Most of the worshipers, particularly the older folk, have arrived and taken their places in the pews. Social conversation ceased when they entered the new sanctuary. They have come early to meditate and pray. Their faces do not register much of the gladness spoken of in the verse from the Psalms, but one senses an unmistakable aura of expectation that God will speak to them in this service. They also anticipate much singing—four to five selections from the choir, as many hymns, and at least two sermons. Worship for these folks is a somewhat too somber affair, but they are convinced of its absolute importance for their spiritual and moral survival. Worship time is an awesome time. *"Gott ist gegenwaertig!"* (God is present!)

Scene 2: A large, international Catholic charismatic convention held in June 1972, at the huge sports stadium of the University of Notre Dame in South Bend, Indiana, on the theme "Jesus Is Lord."

It is Sunday morning—an hour before the public praise and worship service is to begin. Several thousand of the twenty-five to thirty thousand who will gather have already selected their seats in the bleachers. Many of these early birds form small groups to meditate and pray for those who will be singing, speaking, and leading. No doubt, some are also preparing themselves to take communion later that morning. The faces of these people radiate joy, friendliness, and warmth.

The service this morning (which includes the mass) features gifted speakers like Cardinal Suenens of Belgium and one of the most accomplished and dedicated praise and worship music teams in the country. Inspiring and uplifting as their contributions are, the dominant impression of this service is a sense of the presence of the risen Christ in our midst, uniting the thousands of worshipers into a beautiful bond of love and fellowship.

Scene 3: A Sunday morning in January 1975, at the Westminster United Church, Winnipeg, Manitoba.

It is the weekend of the first church music seminar sponsored jointly by Mennonite Brethren Bible College (now Concord College) and Canadian Mennonite Bible College. The world-renowned hymnologist/musician Dr. Erik Routley of England is to preach the sermon this morning. Those of us who have experienced him as a brilliant and entertaining lecturer, talented hymn writer, and musician are more than a little curious how this gifted man will do as a preacher. It is fifteen minutes before the service. Dr. Routley is in the pastor's office, pacing back and forth, head bowed, eyes closed, chin in hand, deep in thought and prayer. He appears to be in a Jacob-type struggle. (He had confided earlier that he skipped breakfast that morning so he could focus on the sermon!) In this service, he delivers one of the most inspiring and powerful sermons I have heard in a decade or so. We experience God-presence this morning through one preacher inspired by God's Word and Spirit and an expectant congregation.

These three very different experiences of preparing for worship embody a primary biblical principle: "As you expect, so shall you receive." God will honor the cry of every waiting, expectant heart. However, the richest and most abundant of God's blessings are released when Christians gather corporately before the service (best in smaller groups) to pray for God's presence and help.

The fast-expanding churches in Africa, Latin America, and elsewhere, including the leaders and worship teams of a local worship center (referred to earlier), consistently gather prior to the service to pray for guidance and empowerment. It is not merely the upbeat contemporary music, the enthusiastic preaching, the drama, and the dancing that draw both members and seekers to such churches. It is the experience of a discernable God-presence that makes attending church a joyous and faith-inspiring experience.

Anticipation of God-presence during worship

A strong sense of expectation of God-presence and the activity of the Spirit should pervade the entire service, but how is it maintained? We know only too well how easily we slip from a praying, expecting mode to a detached spectator mode.

In his stimulating, although somewhat idealistic, little classic, *Prayer: The Mightiest Force in the World,*[19] Frank C. Laubach has a short section entitled "What Happens When a Church Prays?" Here he urges members in the congregation to pray for the pastor **while** he or she speaks. He maintains that when **every** person in a congregation prays intensely **while** the pastor is preaching, instead of viewing the sermon like a spectator who is out to enjoy a good performance, a miracle happens. But it must be unanimous.[20] He also encourages worshipers to send up "flash prayers" for one another.[21] This type of intercession for the pastor and each other may seem idealistic or formula-bound, but its intent is thoroughly biblical and in harmony with our Anabaptist emphasis on the church as the living body of Christ and the priesthood of all believers. Such intercessory prayer has nothing to do with mere piety, but it has everything to do with loving support for the unity of fellowship in Christ. This is, no doubt, an area of worship life, and of church life as a whole, which waits to be reexamined and integrated into worship.

For worship leaders, every part of the service can be enveloped in the blessing of God's presence. The painstaking effort of planning, preparing, and practicing are released in faith to the Lord who is the Spirit. Worship leaders and pastors should be open to the prompting of the Spirit to speak words of encouragement and help relevant to the specific needs of the congregation.

Even the well-prepared music director should be open to fresh intuitions for the interpretation and communication of even the simplest hymn. Never, in a service of worship, should the music director and those singing and playing, regard their singing and music making as the final opportunity to "get things really right." The music of worship is not a glorified religious concert. We take what we have prepared and release it in faith, believing it will be used by God to bless and minister to people. It remains one of the greatest challenges of the music director and those leading the worship music to constantly find that fine balance between concentration on a worthy "performance" and an offering up of oneself as a human agent of spiritual ministry to all those waiting and listening!

Conclusion

This chapter has ended on long-range HOPE in action. This eternal hope motivates anticipation of a **particular** experience of God-presence for the planning, preparing, and participating in a **particular** service of worship. Our long-range HOPE is surely the crucified, risen, and glorified Christ, but the arbiter of hope is the Holy Spirit who enables us to pray for and experience the joy and empowerment of God-presence in the greatest of all undertakings of the human spirit—the worship of our Lord and God. *SOLI DEI GLORIA!*

ENDNOTES

1. David Katz, *Animals and Men: Studies in Comparative Psychology*, 41, quoted in Wohlfahrt Pannenburg, *What Is Man* (Philadelphia: Fortress Press, 1970), 250.

2. Ibid.

3. A classic biblical example is the story of the expectation of Simeon, recorded in Luke 2:25-32. The fulfillment of his hope is highlighted in vv. 29-30: "Master, now you are dismissing your servant in peace, according to your word; for my eyes have seen your salvation "

4. Pannenburg, 52. A recurring phrase in this remarkable book.

5. Harvey Cox, *The Feast of Fools* (Cambridge, Mass.: Harvard University Press, 1970), 126ff.

6. Enlightening from a professional futurologist's viewpoint is the forward to Siegfried Grossmann's *Christen in der Welt von Morgen* (Christians in the World of Tomorrow), (Rolf Kuehne Verlag, 1969).

7. Juergen Moltmann, *Theology of Hope* (London: SCM Press, 1967).

8. Cox, 128, in contradiction to Albert Schweitzer's lifelong preoccupation with identifying the historical Jesus.

9. For Christians, best depicted in Jesus' departing words to his followers, "And remember, I am with you always, to the end of the age" (Matt. 28:20b).

10. Harvey Cox, *Fire from Heaven* (Reading, Mass.: Addison Wesley Pub. Co., 1995), chap. 9ff., "Pentecostalism in Latin America," "We Shall Do Greater Things," p. 161ff., for a delightful report of Cox's visit to a Brazilian pentecostal service.

11. Juergen Moltmann, *The Church in the Power of the Spirit*, (London: SCM Press, 1970), 108-114. In this major work, which appeared ten years after *A Theology of Hope*, Moltmann seeks to show how the Holy Spirit becomes the agent by which hope is kept alive and fruitful for the church.

12. Ibid., 108-114.

13. Cox, chap. 9ff.

14. Moltmann, 110-111.

15. Cox, 161ff.

16. Dietrich Bonhoeffer, *Christology* (Great Britain: Collins Fontana Library, 1960), 27.

17. Karl Barth, *Evangelical Theology: An Introduction* (Great Britain: Collins Fontana Library, 1963), 59.

18. Ibid., 58.

19. New York: Fleming H. Revell, 1946, 31-32.

20. Ibid., 31, 34.

21. Ibid., 38.

Chapter 8

Creative Hymn Singing

by Marilyn Houser Hamm

What you Mennonites do in your congregational singing is what happens in most churches in the choir only.

—Robert Shaw[1]

The words "Mennonite" and "singing"—fine singing—have become synonymous. It is who we are and what we do, what we do well. It is what we love to do.

Who could imagine a group of Mennonites gathering together and not singing?
—Kenneth Nafziger[2]

Traditionally, Mennonites have not thought in analytical terms about congregational singing. It is just something we do. But the fact that we have been doing this thing of singing together week after week, Sunday after Sunday, year after year, generation after generation for literally hundreds of years says much about our doing.

The practice of singing has brought us into community—uniting many voices in the praise and glory of God. We have sung our way through life in all of its experiences. It is in our singing that we have both defined our theology for ourselves and passed it on to our children and to the world. It is in our singing that we meet God. For many of us, it is the primary way that we meet God.[3]

Why do we love singing so much? One reason is because we were born to sing. Our responses often resonate with the poet Maltbie D. Babcock: "All nature sings, and round me rings the music of the spheres."

The "why" and "how" of what music does is difficult to define because it is not tangible. A well-crafted tune lifts a good text far beyond the words themselves. I can speak, "I sing the mighty power of God, that made the mountains rise," but when that text is sung with its counterpart, the powerful tune ELLACOMBE[4] (*Hymnal: A Worship Book*, 46), the mountains rise before me and I touch the power of the God of Creation in the recreated moment. The text has received the breath of life and voice—proclaiming to the world.

The journeying hymns, "So nimm denn meine Hände" (Take Thou My Hand, O Father), "Nun danket alle Gott" (Now Thank We All Our God), "Amazing Grace," "Grosser Gott, wir loben dich" (Holy God, We Praise Thy Name), have become touchstones for life as the stories of our ancestors and our own stories unfold before us. These things, which we know and love, we pass on to our children.

But one more word must be said about this passion for singing among us. In spite of the statements in defense of sound theology and good music that arise, if the truth were to be told, we often sing simply because it is great fun to do so!

"Oh, how we'll make the chorus swell: All is well! All is well!" says William Clayton (*Hymnal: A Worship Book*, 425).

The late-twentieth-century syndrome

How is it, then, that such a church, with such a glorious singing tradition, can be dealing with challenges in the very area of its strength? Gabe Huck, in a wonderful series of essays, states:

We are surrounded by music, but robbed of song.

Certainly, we have music as people have never before had · music. Walk the streets of a city and count the people with stereos in their ears on their way to work, out jogging, working the dog. Make a call, get put on hold, and hear "easy listening" music. Elevator music is a cliché. The supermarket plays music to shop by. . . .

For all the music around us, singing together is no longer part of normal public life, except perhaps the crowd at the ballpark with their very limited repertory. . . .

How shall we sing the Lord's song in a land that is foreign because it robs us of song and soothes us with entertaining music? To sing the liturgy of the church here, now, is to confront life and death. If we treat it as less, we have taken an unworthy path.[5]

Literate and yet illiterate

Our society is considered to be literate, and yet at the same time we read less in general and have in many cases readily thrown away the craft and beauty of language for the sake of instant accessibility and inspiration. In congregational singing, such a tendency has watered down the exciting dynamism of the church's diverse song of many centuries and has created in its stead a pallid, static sound found in "the hymn." Often it is said that we must **do something** to make these hymns more interesting, more creative, as if there were something lacking in the hymn itself.

It is also said, and rightly so, that the song of the church must exist and find its creative expression in every generation. But it is a church narrow in its vision and focus that sees validity only in the present or considers something inspired by the Spirit—which may or may not be truly inspired!

What these all-too-common responses say loudly and clearly is that we have forgotten how to listen. Page after page of the church's song throughout the ages, reflecting the diversity and color of people of many places, times, and languages, have been buried beneath the notes, which have become an end in themselves, rather than merely the beginning of the recreation of the sound that was intended. Being creative with nearly two thousand years of the church's song means that we must begin by RECREATING the sound that was originally intended. We must listen again for the sound that is waiting to be liberated from the page.

Learning to ask questions

The recreative process, says master hymnologist/arranger/composer Alice Parker, must begin with the melody. And from that melody there must come a curiosity that is not unlike that of a human relationship. One asks the melody questions:
- Who are you?
- Where did you come from?
- When were you written?
- For whom?
- Why were you written?
- What vocal or instrumental music was happening in the world around you at the time?

It is in answering these questions that the sound begins to emerge from the page. It is in answering these questions that the black dots on the page begin to have meaning as they serve to make the sound live. The living sound may not be an exact recreation of the original intent, but it will be an informed recreation of the sound that will give it meaning and life. From the melody then, other voices materialize, creating harmony, dialogue, response, and color. A kaleidoscopic vision emerges—a world of discovery and joy, a world of high adventure. To begin, open the door . . .

Taking the recreative approach: six examples

Example 1: "Let the Hungry Come to Me," *Hymnal: A Worship Book* (464)
Text: Sr. Delores Dufner, OSB (Sts 1-3),
Adoro te devote, latens Deitas, 13th c. (sts. 4-5)
Tune: PROCESSIONAL, 1697

One of the earliest musical forms of the Christian church is that of chant or "plainsong," dating from as early as the fourth century ("Holy God, We Praise Thy Name" in *Hymnal: A Worship Book,* 121). A form long forgotten by many traditions and as visually remote as an unfamiliar language, this ancient form has been received with remarkable openness in our spontaneous society. The style of chant with its simplicity evokes a sense of mystery. It requires nothing more than the human voice, human voices in unison. Its serenity evokes awe and reverence—a sense of the presence of the Holy.

Those who experience this musical form find, first of all, that to sing together, we must first breathe together. This common "breath" creates a sensitivity to those around us—a special kind of listening. To sing in this form is an exercise in building community.

The absence of note stems on the page, terrifying to those who strive for rhythmic correctness, is merely a cue that something else is happening here. The "rhythm" of the chant is found by first speaking the text, finding its flowing and lingering points—the words to which others naturally cadence—and then to sing the pitches with that same kind of movement.

Depending on the words to be stressed, the first phrase of this hymn might be sung with a stress on the word "come" as a call:

*Let the hungry **come** to me*

A slightly accelerating movement through the first three words to the word "come," followed by resting on the word "me"—the voice of Christ—creates the sense of the line and a centering on Christ in both text and in the unison pitch.

> **Let** *the poor be fed*

Stressing the word "Let" creates a powerful statement of the will of God in Christ and ultimately a statement of the vision of the church: "Let" these things happen—"do not hinder them."

Key words continue to emerge:

> *Let the thirsty* **come**
> *and* **drink,**
> **share** *my wine and bread.*

Treating the rise in the following line of the notation lightly, rather than with the sense of crescendo to the high point in the phrase, produces a wonderful effect. The symbolism comes through here, the lighter-sung phrase coinciding with the assurance that material wealth is of no importance here. Rather, what matters is the active response to the call:

> **come** *to me and eat.*
> **Drink** *the cup I offer,*
> **feed** *on finest wheat.*

As the congregation sings this hymn, the gathered community becomes the voice of the loving inviting Christ to the world. The expression of the invitation of Christ can be further experienced by dividing the congregation in half to sing alternate lines. A further simple directive to each group to sustain the last note of its phrase while the other group sings creates the sense of the great echoing cathedrals in which this music was first sung. A further sense of timelessness is also created if the leader does not cue the stopping of the sound of the last note. Simply letting the sound become inaudible gives a sense of sound going on through time and space.

Stanzas 4 and 5 become the voice of the community of believers as they sing to one another—affirming their unity in Christ and then offering their corporate prayer to Christ at the close of each of these two stanzas:

Christ our God and brother, hear our humble plea:
By this holy banquet keep us joined to thee.

Example 2:   "In Thee Is Gladness," *Hymnal: A Worship Book* (114)
Text: Johann Lindemann, "In dir ist Freude"
Music: adapt. Giovanni G. Gastoldi,
BALLETTI, 1591

The music of the Renaissance era (roughly covering the years 1450-1600) was filled with lively melodies and energetic rhythmic combinations. "Characteristically, the music was light, fast, set for four voices, syllabic with many repeated notes. . . . They had distinct short sections, which as a rule were repeated so as to form an easily grasped pattern, such as aabc."[6]

The accompanying instruments of the day—recorders in full "consort" or families of three to eight recorders that complemented the full range of human voices; krummhorns (a double-reed instrument), cornetts (made of wood or ivory); trumpets and sackbuts (ancestors of the modern trumpet and trombone but softer in tone); and viols (forerunners of the present-day violin family)—provided the perfect accompaniment for double vocal parts. Added to these were hand drums and percussion instruments.

Recorders, triangle or finger cymbal, and hand drum still create the close accompaniment for this hymn and are readily available. Whether sung in unison or in parts, the singing remains light, quick, and rhythmic. There is no pushing of the vocal sound. One simply "rides the breath" with a feel of one pulse per bar. The movement of the line is toward the long note, i.e., toward "...gladness," "...sadness," "...heart."

The "proper" combination of the tunes and texts, both taken from the time period in which they were written, appeared in *The Mennonite Hymnal* of 1969.[7] It was a delight and a privilege while working on the compilation of *Hymnal: A Worship Book* to hear stories from Professor Mary Oyer of her research in finding these gems. Excitement for these "new" hymns from the 1969 collection ran high as congregations responded to their life-filled, joyous character. Two decades later Mary Oyer reflects that it was precisely the entering of these rhythmic tunes into our canon that profoundly affected the style of our Mennonite singing, making it more rhythmic and precise.[8]

Example 3:   "Be Thou My Vision," *Hymnal: A Worship Book* (545)
Text: Ancient Irish
Music: Irish melody

One of the most beloved additions to the Mennonite canon of hymns in the 1969 *The Mennonite Hymnal* was the Irish hymn "Be Thou My Vision." Recognized instantly for its lyricism and genuine folk beauty and simplicity, it was soon memorized by entire congregations and became a favorite request at hymn sings.

Now, with the *Hymnal Accompaniment Handbook*, congregations have the opportunity to sing this beautiful hymn with a richly fluid piano accompaniment setting by one of the most significant composers/arrangers of our time, Alice Parker. Her genius in sensing the true expression of a melody comes through powerfully in the resetting of traditional, familiar hymns. In introducing this hymn, Alice Parker, with her characteristic sense of humor, encourages congregations to "sing it like you were an Irish tenor."[9] The resulting effect is one of breadth, of expressive line, of lovingly interpreting each word. Some call it "singing your heart out" or "away," because it really becomes a love song.

Example 4: "What Wondrous Love Is This," *Hymnal: A Worship Book* (530)
Text: *Cluster of Spiritual Songs*, 3rd. ed., 1823
Tune: American folk hymn, SOUTHERN HARMONY 1840

The early American folk melodies provide wonderful opportunities for singing in canon and for vocal and instrumental ostinatos (repeated phrases or rhythms). Based primarily on five pitches, the possibilities of entry and reentry by numerous voices are easily achieved without clashes of shifting harmonizations.

The following story is based on this hymn:

There was an inter-Mennonite conference on evangelism some years ago. The song leader for the event had been told only minutes before the beginning of the first worship service that the hymn "What Wondrous Love Is This" had been inserted into the service. Looking at the outline of the service, the song leader realized that the song had no context; what preceded and followed it provided no help in creating the tone for the hymn.

When the time came for the hymn, the leader walked quietly to the piano on the stage and played only the hauntingly beautiful melodic line. Then, leaving the piano, the leader asked the altos and sopranos of the congregation to hum the melody as if it were a distant memory, while the men of the congregation were asked to sustain the pitch E. The women then sang stanza 1 in unison, followed by the singing of the second stanza with increased strength in two-part canon. All the while the men hummed the pitch E.

At the start of the third stanza, the women were asked to leave the melody to begin a vocal ostinato on the pitches B and E with the phrase "I will sing," stressing each pitch. Once the ostinato was securely in place, the men were asked to sing the third stanza with strength in unison. The hymn began to swell, and the people were given a signal to stand. The ostinato continued after the stanza while the leader gave an indication that the fourth stanza could be sung in ostinato voices on the phrase "I'll sing on" or as part of a four-voice canon—each voice entering after the phrase "And when from." What followed was a surging sound, recurring phrases gaining strength from the repetition; wonderful words repeated over and over again, "I'll sing on . . . I'll sing on . . . I'll sing on." The last pitch was sustained by each voice as it arrived at the cadence with full strength and then continued to swell.

The strong cutoff from the director's arm signaled a release that literally sent the sounds echoing into eternity. The director's arms slowly lowered to give the time and space needed to absorb the experience—to breathe and sigh. The singing of that hymn was one of the most powerful faith statements made at that conference.[10]

The singing of a hymn in canon or with vocal or instrumental ostinatos does not just happen. The leader must: (1) know that those possibilities exist; (2) have the exact sound in her ear that she wants to convey; (3) own the style; (4) know the people and have faith that the people can and **will** do what they are asked to do; and (5) have the courage to take the risk. Conducting in two beats per bar, the leader can easily convey to the congregation in a nonverbal way the dynamic level by using a small hand gesture. Ostinatos can also be created, and then played by children on any type of xylophone or glockenspiel.[11]

Example 5:   "In the Rifted Rock I'm Resting," *Hymnal: A Worship Book* (526)
Text: Mary Dagworthy James, *The Chataqua Collection*, 1875
Tune: W. Warren Bentley, THE CHATAQUA COLLECTION, 1875

This beloved hymn of the Russian Mennonites can become a rich and elegant expression of vocal sonorities by having the women and the men of the congregation each sing a stanza in three- or four-part harmony. The directions are as follows:

For women's voices:

I Soprano	- Tenor notes sung one octave higher than written
II Soprano	- Melody
I Alto	- Alto
II Alto	- Bass line sung one octave higher than written

(For three-part harmony, soprano and first alto sing regular parts; second alto sing tenor line at the pitch written.)

For men's voices:

Baritone	- Melody
II Tenor	- Tenor
I Tenor	- Alto line at pitch written
Bass	- Bass

A suggestion for performance would be: all voices, stanza 1; women in parts, stanza 2; men in parts, stanza 3; all voices, stanza 4.

A very simple and yet elegant effect in the overall experience of this hymn may be achieved by putting into place the unwritten-but-well-known practice among church accompanists of playing a hymn notated in four sharps (the key of E major) as three flats (the key of E-flat major). Singing the first three stanzas of the hymn in E-flat major and then using a simple modulation to E major between stanzas three and four gives a very satisfying climax to the fourth stanza. The accompanist should then repeat the final phrase, "I will hide myself in thee," to close the setting.

Example 6:   "Lord, I Want to Be a Christian," *Hymnal: A Worship Book* (444)
Text: African-American spiritual
Music: African-American spiritual

The African-American spiritual is one of the most loved expressions in the church today. Those not of African-American descent often worry about not sounding authentic when they approach these hymns. But actually putting a few key elements into practice can go a long way.

1. The first of these is to **allow time**. Just as the chant form needs the freedom from strict note values, so the African-American spiritual needs the flexibility to stress each word, to not be rushed, and to not let our usual sense of "getting on with the hymn" to avoid dragging the tempo to take over. The effect conveyed here can be described as a very firm foundation—a solid rock that never moves.

2. The African-American tradition is an **aural tradition**, and therefore harmonies and vocal improvisation are merely "heard" and given freedom to enter into dialogue with the melody. There are no right or wrong notes. The singer is free to sing what he or she hears.

This is why the spirituals in *Hymnal: A Worship Book* are presented with the melody line only. It is assumed that congregations will harmonize these pieces, but the freedom to harmonize in any way they like is given by the absence of those parts in notation.

A wonderfully simple but profound way to experience the hymn "Lord, I Want to Be a Christian" is by having a leader sing the first phrase unaccompanied—with congregational voices joining the prayer at the phrase "in my heart." By merely beginning the stanzas at the appropriate volume level, the congregation can be deeply moved in its corporate prayer through this hymn. For example:

Lord, I want to be more loving - at "mp" moderately quiet
Lord, I want to be more holy - at "pp" very quietly
Lord, I want to be like Jesus - at "f" strongly

The accompanist must always be sensitive to the need for breathing places in the vocal line and must sing—if only mentally—with the singers as a reminder of what the vocal line requires. Any phrase, however, for any instrument must have a sense of the breath to define it. With African-American music in particular, allowing space for the breath of the congregation is critical. Accompanists should avoid doubling the solo line in this hymn or should subdue the instruments, so that the subtleties of the vocal inflection and the breath can allow for the strength and power of the Spirit.[12]

The previous examples of wonderful and yet differing styles of music have been suggested for their creative possibilities. They were not meant to be a definitive list by any means, but are presented here to provide a direction—to listen; to look beyond a first glance at the page; to see the breadth, height, depth, and length of the church's song.

There are invaluable treasures in the historical materials of the church. Like our singing, these hymns must be valued and passed on from one generation to the next to be discovered and rediscovered, time and again.

Then the experience that I had in a rural congregation in Zurich, Ontario, in the fall of 1996, can be repeated. During the request time of a service of hymn singing on a Saturday night, at which many children were present, the hand of an eager young nine-year-old boy waved for acknowledgment. As I turned to the boy, expecting a request for a hymn with lively rhythm of non-Western origin, the request came clearly for the hymn "Jesu, Joy of Man's Desiring" (*Hymnal: A Worship* Book, 604). Admittedly stunned and delighted, I turned to his mother who said, "It's his favorite hymn." And so we sang, with Bach's full accompaniment.

In another congregation, where the great hymns of the church were taught to the children in their children's choir, one very little girl exclaimed of the hymn of the day:

I like it because the words taste so good . . .
—and indeed they do!

The church of the present: the song goes on

To deal with the variety and complexity of the music of the late-twentieth-century Christian church would take much more time and space than can be contained within this brief chapter. I would, however, like to raise in brief four observations that for me characterize major threads in the emerging tapestry of the song of the present.

1. There is wonderful crafting of both poetry and music by writers of the present. Some examples in *Hymnal: A Worship Book* are: "What Is This Place" (1); "Wind Who Makes All Winds" (31); "How Shallow Former Shadows" (251); "Open, Lord, My Inward Ear" (140); "Mothering God, You Gave Me Birth" (482).

2. The late-twentieth-century church has been gifted with the music and faith of the global church. The new frontier for the church is to enter into the aural tradition— to sing refrains over and over again; to hear and to create vocal and instrumental parts; to sing from the heart.[13]

3. Instrumentation in the accompaniment of congregational singing has expanded a great deal. Instrumental parts that were formerly reserved for octavos in church choral music files are now readily accessible in *Hymnal Accompaniment Handbook*. Many of our youth as well as adults are studying music and own orchestral or band instruments. The rise of techniques and training in the

methods of Carl Orff in schools has also given rise to wonderful creations of parts for these same instruments (xylophones, metalophones, hand-percussion, recorders), opening the door particularly for the participation of children. Some congregations have acquired their own set of handbells. The guitar song, which emerged in the years just prior to 1969, has found a solid place in the contemporary church's musical expression in a wide variety of stylistic modes. (See Exhibit 1, page 155.)

4. There is a renewed sense in Mennonite churches of the recognition of the role of music in worship as a central action of the gathered community. We are understanding more and more about the functioning of hymns in worship—that when we sing we are praising, proclaiming, praying, confessing, witnessing, etc. What this means for those that plan worship is that the response of the people during the worship experience is heightened if the singing is directly connected to what is happening. Examples of present practice would include the singing of a Scripture text rather than, or in addition to, hearing it in its spoken form. In *Hymnal: A Worship Book*, a response such as the "Alleluia" (101), or "Who Is So Great" (62) provide interaction with and response to the Scripture.

The music of the Taizé community

Amid the vast array of contemporary music available to the church, there is a type of music that does not call for high-tech amplification of instrumental sound or the rhythmic complexity of contemporary notation. It is music that emerged from an ecumenical retreat center for worship in Taizé, France, southeast of Paris. Because the worshipers coming to the Taizé community encompassed many ethnic and geographical origins, there was no common language, either spoken or musical. And so the community sought the assistance of their composer/friend Jacques Berthier, in Paris, to create a "new song" unto the Lord.

With sensitivity and skill, Berthier began the crafting of

melodies and harmonies which were characterized by simplicity, and yet portrayed a beautiful richness of sound and
texture. Repetitive refrains, ostinatos, and canons were
used for the congregation; stanzas were set for soloists or
small groups in a call-response pattern typical of folk
music. Beautiful instrumental parts were written into the
accompaniments for nearly every instrument of the orchestra. The use of these instruments remains flexible, as
instruments are available. But the emerging texture as any
of these parts unfold over the repetitive patterns is one of a
rich tapestry of sound. Those who experience the music of
Taizé find themselves moving from the task of "singing the
hymn" to entering into prayer. There is a sense of timelessness—time to reflect, to meditate, and to meet God and one
another in a frenzied world.

Taizé pieces that are quite accessible from *Hymnal: A
Worship Book* are:

471 "Eat This Bread," a beautiful communion
piece. When sung throughout the distribution of the
bread and cup, many opportunities arise for meditation of
these simple, and yet profound words of our Lord.

242 and 247 "Stay with Me" and "Jesus,
Remember Me" offer opportunities to enter into the biblical drama, and to experience and express our own need.

452 "Ubi caritas et amor" is both an affirmation
and a prayer for unity in Christ.

298 "Veni Sancte Spiritus" inspires the awe and the
life-giving presence of God's Spirit among us.

204 "Gloria." Many opportunities abound here for
children, adults, bells, procession, etc.

348 "O Lord, Hear My Prayer," beautiful and
plaintive; an appropriate response during prayers of great
need.

554 "Our Father Who Art in Heaven" is not simple, but the rewards are great. The congregation's voices
should enter in sequence (bass, soprano, alto, tenor) only
after each voice is securely in place. The leader must be

well prepared to guide the congregation into this experience confidently and with ease. See *Hymnal Accompaniment Handbook* for solo part, which is the sung text of the
Lord's Prayer.[14]

Music from Iona

Beyond our own collections of materials, the music
from the Iona Community in Scotland is providing new
wine in new wineskins for the Christian church in worship
today. Powerful in its focus on the centrality of Christ, passionate in its witness for global justice, and dedicated to
giving the people's song back to a people who have forgotten how to sing or have been told they cannot, the original
music from its writer/composer, John Bell, focuses on traditional Scottish folk melodies or is masterfully crafted
with profound simplicity. As in the pattern of the Taizé
materials, simple melodic phrases are repeated with or
without the addition of sung vocal parts. The music of Iona
differs from the Taizé community in that its focus is primarily the human voice. It does not assume the availabili-
ty of any accompanying instrument at all. The Iona
Community draws largely on the music of the global community for its worship and actively seeks to convey this
richness in its worship and music ministry.

Two examples of worship responses from the Iona collection, "Take, O, Take Me as I Am" and "Behold the Lamb
of God," (Exhibit 2, page 157) are included as worthy representatives and as an invitation to explore this ongoing
rich resource in congregational worship.

Conclusion

I pray that our congregations will continue to grow in
their support of those to whom the task of music ministry
has been entrusted. May God's Spirit continue to lead and
guide us as a church, as a people of God, energizing and
renewing our worship as "through the church the song
goes on."

Exhibit 1

Here is a brief charting on instrumental possibilities and combinations found in *Hymnal: A Worship Book*. The list is by no means comprehensive but will serve as a guide and points to further exploration.

Chart of
INSTRUMENTATION
Hymnal: A Worship Book

Orff Instruments:
   156, 197, 237, 429, 501, 567

Handbells:
   172, 192, 197, 237, 501, 567, 646

Guitar:
   Contemporary Folk: 76, 161, 163, 226, 299, 304, 324, 472
   Country Gospel: 515, 352
   Classical: 34, 88, 314, 361, 441, 594
   Taizé: 242, 247, 348, 554, and others
   Jazz: 372
   Traditional Folk: 427, 441, 562, 623
   Early American: 503, 608, and others
   Folk Anthem: 377, 395, 454, 465, 472, 519, 570, 596, 614
Seasoned guitarists will find this listing to be only the tip of the iceberg. Listings in the following two categories also overlap for guitarists.

Jazz Instrumentation:
   143, 249, 575, 553, 449, 372, 301 (*Acmpt. Hdbk.* 'gospel' version)

Folk Instruments (Guitar, Banjo, Dulcimer, Autoharp, Mandolin, Fiddle):

> 21, 221, 277, 284, 373, 459, 491, 547, 503, many gospel hymns

Brass Instruments:

> Trumpet: 67
> Brass Quartet: 34, 89, 188, 222, 280, 285, 309, 339

Orchestral Instruments:

> Taizé music: 494, 75, 270
> Strings alone: doubling of voice parts, esp. Bach chorales, 471; many hymns

C Instrument Obligatos (Flute, Violin, Oboe):

> 76, 161, 229, 454, 415, 613, accompaniment interludes.

Exhibit 2
Worship Music from the Iona Community:
Two Examples

Take, O Take Me as I Am

Behold the Lamb of God 1

Words: Jn 1:29

Be - hold the Lamb of God, be - hold the Lamb_ of God. _ He

Be - hold   the Lamb, the Lamb   of God. He

takes a - way the sin,   the _ sin ___ of _ the world. ___

takes   a - way   the   sin   of   the   world.

ENDNOTES

1. Robert Shaw to the Mennonite Church Music 280-Voice Chorus, Winnipeg, Man., February 1997.

2. Kenneth Nafziger, *When We Sing: Conversations with Alice Parker & Friends.*

3. Marlene Kropf, Director of Worship and Spirituality for the Mennonite Church. Research among General Conference and Mennonite Church congregations on the significance of hymn singing in their lives, 1997.

4. *Hymnal: A Worship Book* (Elgin, Ill.: Brethren Press; Newton, Kan.: Faith & Life Press; Scottdale: Pa.: Mennonite Publishing House, 1992), 46.

5. Gabe Huck, *How Can I Keep From SINGING? Thoughts About Liturgy for Musicians* (Chicago, Ill.: Liturgy Training Publications). This, along with Alice Parker's *Melodious Accord*, should be in every church musician's personal library.

6. Grout, "New Currents in the 16th Century," *A History of Western Music*, 4th ed. (New York: W. W. Norton & Company, Inc.), 251.

7. *The Mennonite Hymnal* (Scottdale, Pa.: Herald Press, 1969).

8. *Hymnal Accompaniment Handbook* (Elgin, Ill.: Brethren Press; Newton, Kan.: Faith & Life Press; Scottdale, Pa.: Mennonite Publishing House, 1993). See p. 75 for detailed percussion accompaniment for the hymn "In Thee Is Gladness."

9. Alice Parker, Hymn Singing Seminar, Associated Mennonite Biblical Seminary, Elkhart, Ind. Videos: *Yes, We'll Gather at the River: Singing Hymns with Alice Parker* (1993); and *When We Sing: Conversations with Alice Parker and Friends* (1994), produced by Liturgy Training Publications, Chicago, Ill., are available.

10. Marilyn Houser Hamm, Alive '85 Conference, Denver, Colo.

11. Specific suggestions for ostinato patterns for this hymn as well as additional performance possibilities may be found in *Hymnal Accompaniment Handbook*, p. 335.

12. Further suggestions for exploration may be found in the *Hymnal Accompaniment Handbook*, p. 352, or visit your neighborhood African-American congregation! *Hymnal: A Worship Book* offers essays and performance helps on major cultural tradi-

tions of the world.

13. *Hymnal: A Worship Book* offers a fine collection of hymnody. See *Hymnal Accompaniment Handbook* for essays and performance helps on major cultural traditions of the world.

14. See the complete listing of Taizé pieces in *Hymnal Accompaniment Handbook*, p. 434, under Jacques Berthier, or in *Hymnal: A Worship Book*, p. 888.

Chapter 9

Children and Music Ministry

by Jane-Ellen Grunau

It was the Christmas Eve service in a Mennonite church in British Columbia.

> *We are the children of the light!*

One cluster of candles was lit by the children of the grade 5-7 Sunday school class. The church was full.

> *We are the people of the light!*

A second cluster of candles was lit in another corner of the church. The church had now become very still.

> *The light reminds us of the coming of Jesus and the light he brought to earth.*

A third cluster of candles was lit in yet another corner of the sanctuary.

> *The light shines in darkness!* [1]

The final group of candles illuminated the last corner of the church. The children had lit the way.

What a profound beginning to a service remembering the birth of the Christ child. Each word was meaningful and also capable of being echoed by every member of the congregation of whatever age.

The service continued. From the lighting of the candles, this group of children moved to the front of the church, forming a large circle and kneeling with heads bowed. A single voice began to sing:

Come, thou long-expected Jesus

The children's heads slowly rose in response, arms reaching up. The strength of their focus drew the congregation's attention and directed their worship to the simple words:

Born to set thy people free

Still on their knees, they crossed their arms over their hearts and then joyfully reached up in freedom, eyes intent on the heavens.

From our fears and sins release us

Making a gesture as though their heads and arms were weighed down by guilt, the children then joyfully rose as Christ's birth released them.

Let us find our rest in thee

Neighbor found neighbor with outstretched arms, and they slowly moved in a circle, showing us the peace of God's love.

Israel's strength and consolation

Stopping, the children joined hands and raised them together.

Hope of all the earth thou art

Right hands meeting in the center, their eyes unwavering on their joined hands, the children moved around the focal point of Christ, the center of our lives.

Dear desire of every nation

With a small turn, each child was now facing out to us, the congregation of believers, and hands reached out before resting upon their hearts. Until this point, we had been drawn along with them through the powerful poetry of the hymn. Now, in that simple gesture, we had been gathered up and made one.

Joy of ev'ry longing heart.[2]

Each child stepped out of their own circle, reaching out to the members of the congregation. Now we were indeed part of the expression of love that these children were sharing with us.

What an incredible gift of worship the children gave to us that Christmas Eve. Their movement and focus had given us insight into the poetry of the hymn that would not ordinarily have been possible. Is it not our responsibility as the collective church community to encourage each member, of every age, to use his or her gifts to the glory of God as these children had just done?

"Children and Music Ministry" is all about teaching the children in our Mennonite churches by means of example, and through our music, the faith that is so important to us. In order to put this into context, I will first discuss the worship experience of children. In this way we can focus on how to make our music ministry meaningful. From there, I will move into the mainstay of our worship music, the hymn of faith, discussing the importance of finding ways to make both traditional and contemporary hymns accessible to children. While our hymnbooks are not the only sources of quality worship music, the diverse styles of music found within them and the accessibility of these hymnbooks for congregations make them an ideal resource. And finally, we need to teach our children the musical skills necessary for them to be able to explore their gifts as valued members of the church family. When we work toward a mutuality of worship such as this, where the contributions of all ages form the basis of worship, the community is strengthened and enriched, and God is indeed glorified.

Children and worship

Encouraging children to have a vital role in the life of the church, not only enriches the lives of every member of the church community, but also fulfills our duty as teachers and mentors of our children. If they do not have faith in Jesus Christ when they reach maturity, I believe that it is because we as a church have failed to discover a way to teach them our faith and to accept them into the community of believers. We cannot assume that all children who are raised in the church will grow to adopt the faith of their parents. Delegating responsibility for faith development to dedicated Sunday school teachers is not enough. The church must collectively embrace its promise to nurture and teach the children under its care.

> *You shall put these words of mine in your heart and soul, and you shall bind them as a sign on your hand, and fix them as an emblem on your forehead. Teach them to your children, talking about them when you are at home and when you are away, when you lie down and when you rise.* (Deut. 11:18-19)

We are commissioned to raise our children in the way of the Lord in everything that we do. Too often this important task is limited to the home or Sunday school and does not include the church worship service. The worship service is perceived to be for adults and the Sunday school for children. A children's worship time may remove children from the collective worship experience altogether. To fully include our children in the church community, we must integrate them into our worship experience as well. When we bring our children into our worship with meaningful involvement, we are hopefully beginning a lifelong faith journey.

The church community has been called the family of God. In the ideal family, every member is valued. Within our church family, we must strive for a similar ideal. We must try to provide a secure place for our children to learn and experience for themselves the values and beliefs that are important to us. By making the participation in worship a part of the normal life of children, a participation in which their contributions are not only encouraged but valued, children will continue to explore their own beliefs and spiritual needs. When we recognize each individual, regardless of age, as having a valuable contribution to make, we give that individual a unique and special place in the community.

There are many areas in the worship service where the contributions of children can be made with integrity.

- Children on worship teams can have excellent suggestions for hymns and can provide creative ideas for meaningful worship.

- Children can be included in the leading of prayers. Their expressions of love and concern are heartfelt and appropriate.

- Leading worship is a skill that can be taught to interested children and youth by offering sessions specifically to learn this important task.

- The children who have voices that project and who enjoy speaking in public can work at effectively reading Scripture.

- Intergenerational reader's theater can present new insights into the Scriptures.

- Children can learn new hymns and teach them to the congregation.

- The children in your congregation play many instruments. Ask them to accompany the hymn singing.

- Sunday school classes can take turns doing the children's story.

- Ushers of all ages can give out bulletins at the entrance to the sanctuary and collect the offering.

- Children can design bulletin covers.

The possibilities for allowing children to be active participants in the worship service are endless. Although it is less time-consuming to do the work ourselves, the rewards of having children who take ownership in the church and its workings are long-lasting ones.

Providing opportunities for children to become involved in the worship service, where they will be working side by side with members of the church other than parents or Sunday school teachers, will have additional rewards. Such opportunities provide moments to pass on individual faith stories and lifestyles that will lead to friendship and greater understanding.

Children and the hymn tradition

Music has long been an acceptable way to include children in Mennonite church worship services. In the past, the children's choir was often a child's only involvement. The church must also teach children to appreciate the hymns that are part of our church tradition. These hymns provide us with a natural way to pass on faith stories, beliefs, and biblical concepts. The church has worked diligently at collecting worship music with beautiful melodies and harmonies, chosen to reflect texts that are thought provoking and stimulating. We must teach this understanding of musical and theological integrity through an early acquaintance with our hymnbooks.

Teaching children these hymns of faith is, not only a means of passing on our beliefs, but also of tying together the larger Mennonite community by means of a common hymn tradition. Our musical heritage has been an important unifying force within our larger church community of believers. As Mennonites of European heritage, we have been a people who have experienced faith through beautiful four-part harmony singing. The feeling of worship is very powerful when a large group of Mennonites join together to sing their faith. We must examine carefully what we as a Mennonite church need to do to ensure that our children will be able to participate in this continuing tradition in order to benefit from this experience of belonging.

The continued growth of this hymn tradition, as seen in *Hymnal: A Worship Book*, has the potential of connecting us to the larger global community. There are Mennonite communities throughout the world which have developed their own distinctive hymns of faith. In order to use our hymn tradition to tie together this larger community, we must expand our definition of the term *hymn*. The hymn of worship is no longer exclusively one of four-part harmony. The addition of music to *Hymnal: A Worship Book* that is sung by Mennonites in many parts of the world is a positive step in the direction of finding common ground between diverse Mennonite communities. When we make our worship music inclusive of all cultures, we are forging cross-cultural bonds that strengthen the diverse community of believers of which we and our children are a part.

This does not mean, however, that we should forsake our own tradition of singing arrangements of often-complex harmonies. We must continue to teach the skills necessary for children to experience and appreciate our own tradition as well as learning new ones. Teaching worship music from our hymnals that contain many styles of music from all traditions should be a priority. To learn the text and music of hymns in an age-appropriate manner allows children to participate in worship with confidence. It allows them to sing, not only their favorite hymns, but also to have courage to try new ones as well.

Our church schools can aid in this process. I attended a private Mennonite high school, for my senior year. Our music instructor was very serious about his mandate to teach faith through music. While he chose beautiful classical music like Handel's *Messiah* to extend our horizons, he also deliberately focused on the music of the hymnbook, our faith heritage. The hymns we were taught included both the contemporary and the traditional and still number among my personal favorites. It is extremely important for Mennonite independent schools to do their part in educating young people toward musical integrity that includes both old and new styles of music.

Over the years, I have tried to examine what makes a hymn a favorite for me and, by extension, which hymns will become favorites for our children. I have come to the conclusion that favorite hymn selections revolve, not only around integrity of music and text, but also around our personal understanding and familiarity with that music and text. That is where church musicians come in. If the children under our care are to embrace our love of church music and carry it forward to the next generation, we must first teach them to understand it. To understand the importance of our church music, children must be involved in making it. Again, this takes time and effort, but the rewards are great. As my son recently said, "I didn't like this hymn until I played it on my bassoon." For my son, the connection to that particular hymn was through his musical instrument. It is our job to make these connections happen.

Children and music education in the church

Our churches must encourage new growth within our musical tradition. This is only possible if the necessary skills are in place. In the past, our children have received a certain amount of musical education in the school system which we, as church musicians, could use and build upon. Due to budget cuts in many school divisions, music programs have been significantly reduced or have even disappeared. To fill this gap, we must provide some form of musical education within our churches. Children's choirs can be one form of musical education which will further our children's musical skills.

Our time of singing on Sunday mornings will also, of necessity, need to become a time of music education as well as worship. There are educational reasons as well as those of faith and tradition for singing from the hymnbook. The children will become familiar with the concepts of reading music, singing in harmony, and being part of a musical ensemble. To learn to harmonize is to be able to explore the wonderful church music that has been written to glorify God throughout the ages. To learn to harmonize is also to have the skills to explore the many dimensions of music from other Mennonite cultures that are often outside of our realm of expertise. Making a wide variety of quality church music familiar to the children and youth of our churches needs to be an important part of their Christian education. Children need to be taught an appreciation for well-written music.

When we teach children to sing challenging music, we also encourage an atmosphere that invites a mature creative response from our own community of composers and poets. This response provides thought provoking and meaningful music for our contemporary worship needs. We have a wealth of talent within the Mennonite community. If we are able to retain and encourage a strong musical, literary, and cultural heritage, we will have the necessary means to pass on our values and beliefs from one generation to the next.

I believe that hope for both the present and the future lies in educating, not only our children, but also in allowing them to educate us as well. Our family spent close to twenty years as members of a church in which our children had the benefit of direct musical involvement in both the worship service and in separate singing times from the time they were toddlers all the way through high school. The children of this church actively participated in all aspects of the musical life of the church and their contribution was valued. The result was a group of people in their teens that were excited about sharing their musical gifts with the church. They had worked with music from the sixteenth century through to the present and had learned to appreciate the best music of each style. Through their appreciation for a balance of musical expression, these young people were also able to teach an appreciation of new musical styles to the congregation. These young people used their music to further their faith, and this inspired every other member of the worshiping community.

The gifts of these young people had been recognized and given value by the church community, and as a consequence they felt a part of that community. The spiritual and emotional bonds of growing up in such an inclusive faith community will remain with them forever.

Children and their gift of music

An appropriate philosophy of teaching music to children, which could be applied within the context of Mennonite churches, is found in the approach of Carl Orff (b. Munich 1895). The Orff approach uses a combination of singing, speech, movement, and the playing of instruments focusing on direct, creative involvement rather than on passive rote learning. As Helen Kemp has said "Body, mind, souls, and voice—it takes the whole person to sing and rejoice!"

Orff combines active participation with a creative mixture of musical experience. Metric speech and rhythmic phrases can be used as interesting ways to experience biblical passages. Psalms and stories, recited to a beat using snapping fingers, clapping hands, and "patching knees" (called body percussion) are, not only fun to learn, but also help children to retain the content because they can experience the learning through movement as well. Having children develop their **own** body percussion and melodic ideas will stimulate their creative thinking and promote positive emotional development. They have been given the permission to create, and their ideas are being valued. The confidence that comes with expertise will grow stronger, making them willing to participate and to share of themselves.

Creativity is a strong component of the Orff philosophy of music education. Children are encouraged to improvise their own melodies to biblical texts and ideas. They are asked to create movement for hymns to help them learn the meanings of the words. Their insights can in turn teach us new ways of looking at those same biblical texts.

An excellent example of this occurred when my grade 1-2 Sunday school class learned the canon "Jubilate Deo omnis terra" (*Hymnal: A Worship Book*, 103). The text is in Latin, so there was little or no understanding of the text for the children or for the many adults who may not have looked at the bottom of the page for the translation. We learned this canon, using movement to help us understand the meaning of the text.

Jubilate Deo (rejoice, all ye lands) started with our bodies bent low, bursting up high to rejoice with our hands moving in a rolling movement up to God until we were standing up tall, hands and eyes directed up to the heavens.

Omnis terra (all the nations are rejoicing, from sea to sea) was sung with both hands beginning at the right side, and the left hand moving across the body to the left, our eyes following it, as if moving around the world.

Servite Domino (serve the Lord) started with our hands flat, palms up, pretending to be a platter of food which moved up as an offering to God.

In laetitia (with gladness) had our hands moving joyfully upward once more as with *Jubilate*.

Alleluia, Alleluia was sung with our bodies stretched up and moving from side to side to become the palm branches that waved when Jesus entered Jerusalem.

In laetitia. Alleluia, Alleluia, in laetitia.

Variations of the following repeated patterns (called ostinati) were played by the children throughout the hymn on the alto glockenspiel (AG, small barred instrument with metal bars), alto xylophone (AX, medium-sized barred instrument with wooden bars), and the bass xylophone (BX, large barred instrument with wooden bars). These instrumental patterns had been developed and refined by a number of children's groups in the past few years. (Due to the creative license of the children, these parts are generally different each time they are played.) They were learned using simple word patterns ("Will you be my friend" and

"Yes, I will") that were found by the children to fit the rhythm of the ostinati. A few Sundays later, the class taught this canon to the church. The children explained the text, illustrating it with their movement, encouraging the congregation to join them. The congregation then sang it once with all the instrumental parts and the movement. Then smaller groups of children led sections of the church in singing the hymn in parts, accompanied by only the alto glockenspiel and bass xylophone parts.

Jubilate Deo #103

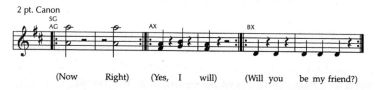

(Now   Right)   (Yes, I   will)   (Will you   be my friend?)

In the course of learning this hymn, the children had accomplished a number of things. They had worked on the mechanics of music, through experimenting with beat, rhythm, melody, movement, instruments, and their own creativity. They became well acquainted with one of the new hymns in our hymnbook. Through the movement, the children were able to understand what they were singing, as were the other members of the congregation. They had played a vital part in the musical worship of that Sunday, and they had been enthusiastically affirmed for their contributions.

Through this experience, the children were respected for who they were—children, not miniature adults or prospective choir members. Their unique contributions as children had been accepted and appreciated as they brought their **own** gifts to God as part of the community's worship experience. Their response touched everyone present. The children had also felt the power that comes from joining their individual voices and actions with the worshiping community. I believe that this mutuality of worship is the key to the ongoing life of the church.

The celebration of mutual ministry

A few weeks ago, we sang the hymn "Jesu Joy of Man's Desiring" (*Hymnal: A Worship Book*, 604) in church, but not in the usual way. Using the *Hymnal Accompaniment Handbook*, the pianist played the beautiful chorale prelude by J. S. Bach. Where the hymn tune appeared, the congregation sang in four-part harmony accompanied by a seventeen-year-old oboist, a thirty-five-year-old clarinetist, a twelve-year-old French horn player, and a fourteen-year-old bassoonist. The majesty of the hymn was felt by all. We could reflect upon the text during the interludes played by the piano. The intergenerational music group had helped us reach a deeper worship experience than would have been possible with only the piano, and through it all, the music group had developed a greater appreciation for the hymn as well.

We have much to learn from children. Jesus showed us this through his example:

> *People were bringing little children to him in order that he might touch them; and the disciples spoke sternly to them. But when Jesus saw this, he was indignant and said to them, "Let the little children come to me; do not stop them; for it is to such as these that the kingdom of God belongs. Truly I tell you, whoever does not receive the kingdom of God as a little child will never enter it." And he took them up in his arms, laid his hands on them, and blessed them.* (Mark 10:13-16)

While we have often heard that children are our future, we must remember that even more importantly, we, as an intergenerational community, are experiencing worship in the present. When Jesus taught the adults who gathered about him, he encouraged them to become childlike in their faith.

In *The Testimony and Prayer of Three Anonymous Children,* John L. Bell writes:

> *When I was a child,*
> *I gave him all I had.*
>
> *He stood among hungry people*
> *who needed food.*
> *And I believed that he knew*
> *how to make the food go round.*
> *Now that I am an adult,*
> *I have much more to share.*
> *But, though the crowds are still hungry,*
> *I am reluctant to give him what I have.*
>
> *Lord, when today I see the face of those*
> *who long for food and justice,*
> *when I hear their cry,*
> *make me as generous as when I was a child.*[3]

Through the involvement of children, we can observe the purity of their motives, their innocence, their boundless potential, their instinctive understanding of truth, and their unquestioning faith. Their trust and simple faith can be reminders to us all to rely on our faith when life becomes complicated.

Before Easter, I taught my grade 1-2 Sunday school class a Nigerian hymn, "In Your Sickness" (*Hymnal: A Worship Book*, 585):

> *In your sickness, your suff'rings, your trials, and pains,*
> *he is with you all the time.*
> *Persecution, temptations, and loneliness,*
> *he is with you all the time.*
>
> *He is there with you, he is there with you,*
> *he is with you all the time.*
> *He is there with you, he is there with you,*
> *he is with you all the time.*

We were completing a unit that consisted of the stories of Jesus, leading up to the time of Easter. We discussed the text of the hymn. We looked for examples in our own lives of people who were suffering, who were sick, who had trials, and who were in pain. As a small congregation, we have all felt pain very keenly when one of our own is suffering. We talked about people we knew who were persecuted, who were faced with temptation, and who were lonely. In spite of their young age, these children could identify with the words of this hymn. We then combined the text with the music. What struck me immediately was the happiness with which the children sang this song. It was a song of grief and suffering, but what the children focused on were the lines,

> *He is there with you*
> *He is there with you*
> *He is with you all the time ...*

We added maracas, wood blocks, and bongo drums, and the effect was one of unquestioning hope and trust. It was simple. God is with us all the time. This was what we shared with the congregation during a service of worship.

The grade 5-7 Sunday school class mentioned at the beginning of this chapter will never forget the words to "Come, Thou Long-Expected Jesus." They will also never forget the insights they gained into the theology of the hymn after working through the movement. They will be able to join with many worshiping communities to sing their faith. But they have also had the opportunity of sharing a faith experience with the congregation by leading them in a meaningful time of worship.

A quote was recently passed on to me, and I appreciate its message. "When we speak about young people in our churches, we tend to focus on the 'young' rather than on the 'people'." When we move the emphasis to 'people,' the perspective becomes more inclusive:

We are the children of the light!

We are the people of the light![4]

As members of the church community, our children have a voice capable of expressing hope, disappointment, individual needs, and insights on many levels.

It is the mutual ministry of children and adults within the church that we must celebrate and affirm. The roles of ministering and also of being ministered to are parts of the same whole. To be the recipient of our children's ministry is to give the gift of acceptance and worth. To be the recipient of our children's ministry is also to move toward wholeness of worship and wholeness of faith.

It was now almost the end of the Christmas Eve service.

The old man in the spotlight watched the boy with the drum who was . . .

> *Waiting . . .*
> *waiting to play . . .*
> *waiting for some signal*
> *that now is the time for music*
> *   now is the time to rejoice*
> *and herald another treasure*
> *come into the world*
> *newly shaped*
> *by the music of the stars*[5]

From another part of the sanctuary came a lone voice reading Luke 2:1-20.

> *In those days a decree went out from Emperor Augustus*
> *that all the world should be registered . . .*

As the story was being read, the youth rose and moved to the periphery of the congregation. The two young people closest to the clusters of candles in the back corners of the church lit their own candles. On each side of the church the light was passed, from friend to friend. As the light passed, the youth moved forward to surround the sanctuary of people. In turn, they spoke the words:

> *You give us light, Lord,*
> *light to see the pain in another person's heart . . .*
>
> *light that can shine through us to people everywhere.*
>
> *Light our paths, O God,*
> *light our lives with your love . . .*
>
> *As the stars shine on the miracle of Christ's coming,*
> *so they shine on us today.*
>
> *We are children of the same light that shone on*
> *Bethlehem.*
> *We are followers of the Christ who came to earth as a*
> *baby.*
>
> *Together we covenant to share the bread of life, the*
> *Christ, with others.*
> *Together we greet the season of joy,*
> *mindful of the fulfillment of Christ's life, in the cross.*
>
> *You are the bread of life,*
> *the star that heralds new life,*
> *and the light of the world.*
>
> *You are the bread of life,*
> *the star that heralds new life,*
> *and the light of this most silent night.*[6]

We sang "Silent Night" illuminated by the light of our youth. I was not the only member of the church moved by the testimony of faith that had united us as one community of believers.

ENDNOTES

1. Taken from "Of Light, Bread & Stars," a Christmas program written by Lynette Wiebe, with music and movement by Jane Grunau and Ruth Krentz, December 1996. This program may be found in the Resource Centre, 600 Shaftesbury Blvd., Winnipeg, MB R3P 0M4.

2. *Hymnal: A Worship Book* (Elgin, Ill.: Brethren Press; Newton, Kan.: Faith & Life Press; Scottdale, Pa.: Mennonite Publishing House, 1992).

3. John L. Bell, "He Was in the World," taken from *The Testimony and Prayer of Three Anonymous Children* (Chicago, Ill.: GIA Publications, 1995), 75.

4. Wiebe, Grunau, and Krentz, "Of Light, Bread & Stars."

5. Ibid.

6. Ibid.

Chapter 10

And What Shall We Do with the Choir?

by Kenneth Nafziger

The special function of leaders or groups in the music of worship is common throughout the history of music in the church. Care for the musical aspects of worship reaches back to the earliest days of the Hebrew people when, already in Genesis 4, we read the accounts of how the descendants of Methuselah apportioned the work of the tribe:

> *Lamech took two wives; the name of the one was Adah, and the name of the other Zillah. Adah bore Jabal; he was the ancestor of those who live in tents and have livestock. His brother's name was Jubal; he was the ancestor of all those who play the lyre and pipe. Zillah bore Tubal-cain, who made all kinds of bronze and iron tools.*

When the ark of the covenant finally found a permanent resting-place in the splendor of Solomon's temple, one family was set apart to be the musical "priests" of the tribe:

> *David and the officers of the army also set apart for the service the sons of Asaph, and of Heman, and of Jeduthun, who should prophesy with lyres, harps, and cymbals. . . .*

> *All these were the sons of Heman the king's seer, according to the promise of God to exalt him; for God had given Heman fourteen sons and three daughters. They were all under the direction of their father for the music in the house of the Lord with cymbals, harps, and lyres for the service of the house of God. Asaph, Jeduthun, and Heman were under the order of the king. They and their kindred, who were trained in singing to the Lord, all of whom were skillful, numbered two hundred eighty-eight. And they cast lots for their duties, small and great, teacher and pupil alike.* (1 Chron. 25:1, 5-8)

And when the temple was finally dedicated, the results were astonishing:

> *Now when the priests came out of the holy place (for all the priests who were present had sanctified themselves, without regard to their divisions, and all the levitical singers, Asaph, Heman, and Jeduthun, their sons and kindred, arrayed in fine linen, with cymbals, harps, and lyres, stood east of the altar with one hundred twenty priests who were trumpeters). It was the duty of the trumpeters and singers to make themselves heard in unison in praise and thanksgiving to the Lord, and when the song was raised, with trumpets and cymbals and other musical instruments, in praise to the Lord, "For he is good, for his steadfast love endures forever," the house, the house of the Lord, was filled with a cloud, so that the priests could not stand to minister because of the cloud; for the glory of the Lord filled the house of God.* (2 Chron. 5:11-14)

To which Johann Sebastian Bach, in the margins of his Bible at verse 13 wrote, "Where there is devotional music, God with His grace is always present."

The role music plays here, this offering of sound, this moving of the Spirit among the people, is at the heart of any discussion about the relationship between music and worship for our time.

As with all other aspects of worship these days, the role and function of the church choir are constantly being reviewed. In times of change, it is good to engage ourselves with these questions of change in the context of broader themes, values, and practices. This chapter seeks to explore a number of questions that concern church choirs: placement in the service, function in worship, repertoire, the formation of ensembles, the relationship with the other members of the congregation, and the pastoral role of the choir in ministering through music in worship. In addition to specific questions related to church choirs, there is also the larger question about the function of the choir as a teaching body. Given all the new musical languages that are available for singing in worship, there is a danger of doing the new with the same or similar musical inflections that we applied to the old and familiar. In other words, all our church music runs the risk of sounding like chorales, or gospel songs, or some other familiar musical style. Someone—most likely the choir—will need to assume major responsibility for shaping the way music is made for the next generation.

What is the liturgical function of a choir?

The choir is an integral part of the liturgy of worship. This liturgical function includes priestly responsibilities, in which acts on behalf of the congregation or on God's behalf are carried out, or where the singing of the choir has a particular role in shaping and articulating the flow and the rhythm of the service.

For many, the choir offers "special" music that enriches worship. Choral music offers worshipers an opportunity for more passive involvement, sometimes touching the head, or the heart, or a part of the body, calling forth reaction, but no overt response. Therefore, the choices in choral music and the use of a choir in worship affect many other aspects of worship. When any of the choices become automatic or expected, they lose something of their significance, appearing for their own sake, not for the sake of worship, or worshipers, or even for the art of music. A number of factors need to be considered in this regard.

The most significant music of worship must be congregational song. Song for the worshiper gives voice to that which is known but not understood; it opens the soul to the movement of sounding breath and body and beauty and provides an unequaled moment of creativity. Nothing, absolutely nothing, should take away from this special, very sacred, and often sacramental aspect of participation for the worshiper. The congregation deserves consideration as a choral singing body. To replace their singing with the singing of the choir would be a reversion to pre-Reformation patterns of music in worship, where the choir sang the liturgy and the worshipers did as they pleased, pausing in reverence only at the sounding of the Sanctus bell.

The choir's calling is not, therefore, to take over the responsibilities of the singing congregation, apart from the question of how well or how poorly the congregation sings. Many are driven to distraction when a choir sings something the congregation could sing, were they invited to do so. It is insulting to have the choir be a substitute for congregational song solely on the grounds that the choir can do it better. The sound of a singing congregation bears little resemblance to the significance of the act of singing itself. Caution should be exercised so that if and when a choir sings, their singing is not subtracted from the amount of time the congregation has for singing.

There are ways of using choral music that do not detract from the congregation's song. The choir can function as an important teaching body for the congregation. There are many new hymns in the current generation of hymnals that ask much of the congregational singer. In addition, all the new hymnals offer the possibility of singing in a much more diverse array of styles than those found in old hymnals. To be able to sing from a book that includes the musical languages of over a thousand years of Christian experience plus the musical languages of an expanding international Christian community is both an opportunity and a challenge. Choirs can act as powerful models in teaching their congregations.

There are many ways of using a choir as a leader that ultimately invite the congregation's participation. There are many choral concertatos available, works based on familiar hymn tunes with elaborate and colorful instrumental accompaniments, interesting and demanding choral parts, the addition of children's or youth choirs, and opportunities for the congregation to join in. Philosophically this is a good and practical way of viewing one of the choir's functions within its congregation. The sacred cantatas of Johann Sebastian Bach offer another practical model for the use of choirs in relationship to congregations. Many of his cantatas have their most complicated work at the beginning; there is no question but that this is choral music. (Sometimes, this complicated choral activity is based on a hymn tune of the time.) At the end of the cantata, one usually finds a four-part choral setting. While it is not likely that Bach's congregation would have sung this, the point is that they could have, had they been provided with the notation. The tune and text were drawn from the common body of hymns of eighteenth-century Lutheran Leipzig. The harmonization, always designed around the text, was supported by doubling wind and string instruments. The important points that are applicable (and adaptable) to the use of choral music in modern worship are these: The beginning is the more complex. The ending is simple. The connection to congregational song is strong. The function within the total worship experience of the day is clear.

There are important questions to consider when choosing whether or not to use a choir in worship: What is it that a choir can bring to the worship experience on a particular day that nothing else could do as effectively? And what is it that the choir can do for the congregation that it cannot do for itself at a given moment in worship? At times, a choir might be able to sing and speak things that are beyond the congregation's ability to sing or speak, either because of appropriateness or technical difficulty. At other times, the need on the part of a congregation for passive participation can offer a respite from the intensity of involvement. Still other times, there may be the need for choral music because the congregation needs to do something else during the time the music goes on, including moving to another place, offering gifts, or praying. And there are times when the congregation needs pastoral help and support in learning new hymns and in learning how to sing better. If one considers the graciousness that hospitality requires of guests in our homes and applies those considerations to worship, relationships between choir and congregation can be both warm and nourishing.

Entertainment, as the word is used in reference to music and the other arts, has come to be equated with distraction, something that will take away our attentiveness, our receptivity, and something that will alleviate the otherwise dreary and heavy aspects of our lives. This understanding is particularly offensive in the context of worship. If worship brings the community of believers into the presence of God, to look as clearly as possible into the face of God, to speak as directly as possible into the ears of God, and to hear as intelligibly as possible the Word God has for the community, there is no time or place or need for distraction. The work of worship planning should preclude distracting entertainment.

The writer of the letter to the Hebrews, referring to the story of the angels who visited Abraham, says, "Remember to show hospitality. There are some who, by so doing, have entertained angels without knowing it." Entertainment rightly understood as hospitality is a profound and important function in the life of the church, even though it often receives too little attention. To care hospitably for the needs of the worshiper will help us all to keep a proper perspective on the importance of what each of us contributes to worship. In the case of choral music, the question about for whom the choir and choral music exist finds a helpful answer from the example of entertaining angels without knowing it.

Where shall the choir be in worship?

There are choices to be made concerning the physical place of the choir in worship that significantly affect how the music is experienced by the performer and how the music is received and understood by the worshiper. No choice is without difficulty; none is absolutely ideal. All of these are made either easy or somewhat challenging by the architectural design of the space. Aspects of worship need to be considered in relation to the place of the choir and the best option chosen for each congregation.

If the choir is located at the front of the worship space facing the worshipers, either directly or at an angle, there are several immediate advantages. First of all, having the choir in front makes the leading of congregational singing an easy and natural matter. What the congregation gets back when they sing is the sound of singing, the sound of voices coming back to them. For worshipers who are not always secure in their singing, it is reassuring when other voices are heard filling in the gaps around the insecure ones, supporting their efforts to join a congregation of singers. This physical arrangement can be helpful in minimizing the damage done to singing in acoustically dead surroundings. If the choir is located at the front of the worship space, there is a visual completeness to the congregation, a roundedness that provides a visual sense of community. On the other hand, having the choir at the front also offers the most opportunity for distraction: dress, sneezing, the need to circulate information within the choir about changes in plans, any inattentiveness to the actions of worship (especially when the choir is not involved), and others. The choir, when seated (or standing) in the front of a body of worshipers must always be aware that everything it does is crucial to the way the members of the congregation are led in worship.

A second option would be to locate the choir at the rear of the worship space, either on the same level with the rest of the congregation or in a balcony. This option offers many of the advantages cited above with the additional benefit of anonymity. When the singers in the choir and/or the musicians in the orchestra are not seen, the resulting disembodied sound is attractive to many people. Concentration on what the music conveys to them is made easier. For many the hiding of all the activity that happens during a choral/instrumental performance is desirable.

The greatest singular disadvantage of having the choir at the back or out of sight is that the singers in the choir can too easily feel separated from the rest of the congregation. Hidden in obscurity, only now and then to emerge to contribute to the worship experience, they may be able to get a lot of other work done, but this is not the intention of worship.

A third option for the placement of the choir in worship is to consider the choir as members who come from within the congregation, who move from being members of the worshiping body to being members of a worship leading body (the choir) by walking from their places in the congregation to lead in singing and then returning to those places. This choice offers a number of valuable advantages. In the first place, singers in our Mennonite congregations have come to prefer sitting with family groups and/or friends during worship. Allowing singers to come out from their places respects those preferences. Another consideration is the visible symbolic act of a choir or any other group or individual coming from within the congregation to function within their special calling in worship and then again taking their places within the body. For some, all this motion (or commotion) will be an important symbolic statement; for others it may achieve little more than distraction.

Questions about attire do not need to be dealt with here. Several important philosophical and symbolic considerations that lie behind each of the options are contained in these questions:

1. Is the choir a completely separate body from the rest of the congregation?
2. Is the choir a representative selection of members drawn from the congregation?
3. Is the identity of the choir maintained through its visual appearance? Or is its visual appearance only one of its marks of identity? Are there other (or additional) means by which an ensemble can develop an identity?
4. How do the individuals relate to one another and to the group? Is one expected to surrender individual identity for the identity of the group?
5. How do the visual aspects of uniformity / diversity affect the entire visual landscape of a worship space? What about choices of color and style in terms of their contributions to the total visual quality of the space?

With reference to all these questions of placement and attire, the ultimate concern must be for the effect that the choices have on those who come to worship. The choices made by a congregation will likely be different from what they would be in a concert situation. They all have important ramifications for other aspects of worship. None of the decisions ought to be left to chance (receiving little or no consideration) or to custom (inviting worshipers to take things for granted). Each congregation with its own space has several possible options, each of which can strengthen and support the quality of worship in very particular ways.

How does the choir educate the congregation?

The important role of the choir in modeling sound cannot be overstated. The demonstration of good singing which the congregation can learn from and follow is of much greater value than a lecture on how things should be done. The pastoral quality of the work of the choir is often overlooked. An invitation to sing in new styles and forms must be warm and trustworthy. The choir often replaces the director (in the Mennonite Church tradition) or the organist (in the General Conference tradition). The choir that functions pastorally for its congregation teaches by shared experience. Such a choir will be sensitive to the vast array of choral sounds, tone qualities, and musical languages that are represented in contemporary hymnals. It will assist in the musical life of the members of its congregation, enabling them to do things they never thought they could do, to go places in their singing they thought they would never go.

A choir can help establish a musical standard for its congregation. Tastes in choral music often appear to be no more than those of the director. There is more than meets the ear here. We seem to be living in a time when people are less willing to devote the time needed to rehearsing choral music. Every congregation and every community has so many choices available to them that there is never enough time to do things as well as they deserve to be done. The quality of the congregation's music stands to suffer when it becomes clear to the congregational singers that there is less expected of the choral singers, signifying that what was once of great importance does not matter as much anymore. Hymn singing, once considered irreplaceable—a matter of importance or even of pride—will no longer serve such an important role.

The choir, in many instances, has an important responsibility to teach the congregation to use its voice, or in the worst cases, to find the voice it has lost. In our culture less and less time is spent singing, even though we have access to some of the finest singing from all over the world recorded by means of the most current technologies of sound reproduction available. We are fast becoming spectators, even in worship, forsaking the unique involvement which singing provides us with. Choirs, in some instances, may even need to remind their congregations of the preeminence of the voice over instrumental or vocal harmonized sound and, most especially, over amplified sound.

John Bell, of the Iona Community in Scotland, often works in churches where singing has almost ceased, where people no longer believe they have a voice. His work is a powerful reminder to those of us who have not yet lost the tradition of congregational or choral singing. Based on his experience, he tells us that there is nothing more laudable than a congregation learning to sing a melody well in unison. His advice speaks especially to those smaller congregations who would like to have a choir but don't believe they have the resources to create one.

Among Mennonite Church congregations in years past, there was a fear that were the church to admit organs into its sanctuaries, all hope would be lost for congregational singing. Little did they know that when, instead of organs, guitars, with guitarists untrained for leading music in worship, came, it would have the same feared result. The guitar in and of itself is a wonderful instrument with much fine repertoire. It was the accompanying need for electronic amplification and louder and more aggressive playing, following trends set in popular music, that robbed the singing voice of its central place in worship. The individual human voice, and even a congregation of voices, has very little chance against amplified sound. Those who sing with the assistance of microphones have an unfair advantage over those who do not. Electronically amplified sound is dependent on mechanics and technology. Music depends for its sound on a resonating body, the ideal for this being the human body. Those who like the effects of electronically produced sounds on their bodies mistake the beating of sound on the exterior of the body for the resonance that comes from within a sounding body. The two do not affect the body in the same way. In addition, electronically amplified sound has the ability to render congregational singing useless in ways that even the loudest of acoustic instruments has not managed.

Most importantly, music in worship is about singing. Whatever we can use to enrich the singing—harmonies, choirs, instruments—should be used, but their use should support the needs of those who worship that they may continue to use the voices they have.

How do we talk about repertoire?

The question of what the choir should sing is an important and difficult one. It has become difficult to stay informed concerning new publications, especially from the standard and established publishing houses. (Some would argue that this is so because churches have so grievously misused copy machines to save themselves some money, thus driving up both cost and easy access.) It is unfortunate that the free materials (including tapes) that are mailed widely are not necessarily representative of the best in new choral music. We live with the overwhelming influence of the popular Christian media who have very skillfully defined their ideas and concepts about both worship and music in a narrow and restrictive way.

It is incumbent upon the responsible church musician to look beyond that which is readily available and to be informed of the breadth of choices. The wisdom accumulated by those experienced in choral music in the church should be respected. Listening to the voices of experience should be combined with attention to the wide variety of music available. Often there is no better way to learn new insights than by attending and participating in choral reading workshops. The Mennonite denomination would do well to assume some responsibility for workshops designed with attention to the uniqueness of our theology and the importance of our singing tradition.

A choir also has an additional responsibility as the keeper and protector of the crown jewels of the church's sacred music. It needs to function as a repository of sacred music. The standard cantata, motet/anthem, and oratorio literature has, for the church, been a rich resource of beauty, theology, and craft. Despite those who would easily discard it all in favor of whatever happens to be popular at the moment, the church should, without question, preserve this resource. Looking only to the past is a sign of a body that is dying; holding only to the future is a sign of rootlessness; and a view of time in which nothing other than the present moment is of any significance is ill-advised and shortsighted.

There are several ways in which a choir program can act as a lively repository. In the first place, much of the oratorio and cantata literature is beyond the capabilities of many individual church choirs. One solution is obvious: cooperation. Congregations that cooperate in big musical projects now and then can make just as strong a statement to our fragmented world as we make with our Mennonite Central Committee Relief Auctions. In addition, many communities have people in them who would not think of darkening the door of a church for worship but for whom music has become a primary avenue by which an encounter with the divine is sought. This is an outreach that congregations often overlook, perhaps because music for Mennonites is so much a part of church life. The instruction from Jesus in the great commission was to proclaim the gospel, which is different from simply expanding the church membership roles.

The standard oratorio and cantata repertoire is musically demanding for many singers whose primary venue for choral singing is the church choir. The tendency of present-day culture would be to shun this sort of a challenge in favor of quick success and less strenuous effort in achieving a finished product. Just as the body does not grow in strength by exercising less or by reading books about exercising, neither does the art or science of singing get better by lowering the demands made on the intellect, body, and soul. Access to great recordings of this literature is nearly unlimited and should be utilized. Many listeners can spend money for tickets to hear this great music in some of the greatest halls in the world, and this resource for music is also important. It is a potentially disastrous mistake of our time to assume that we can leave music making only up to those who can do it better than we can, or that if we pay enough money we can have perfection. This music belongs to the church; the church ought to embrace it with open arms rather than sending it away from its door. (Is it, after all is said and done, the music of the church that's been the prodigal, or is it the church?)

Another possibility that should be explored is the use of these crown jewels in worship. An enormous amount of this cantata literature was written expressly for worship purposes, and to leave it to the domain of the concert hall tears it from its context. Johann Sebastian Bach's use of the church cantata may be instructive for us. In the service of his time, the cantata acted as the musical partner of the sermon. It was a musical exposition on the gospel reading of the day. Worshipers in those churches heard, in effect, two very powerful viewpoints on the Scripture: a sermon and a musical composition. (Worshipers came to St. Thomas in Leipzig from great distances because the church was renowned for the richness of its worship, a radical contrast to today's entertainment venues that attract large crowds.) The larger question raised by these Bach cantatas is this: How can the music, prepared and performed (by choir, soloists, and orchestra), find a context within the worship service that will allow the music to complement the other elements of worship and to reach many individuals in differing ways, while also allowing the other elements of worship to complement the music? This broad question has to do, not only with choices of choral music for worship, but also with how one composes church music that does in our time what Bach's music did in his.

Conclusion

"Where there is devotional music, God with His grace is always present" (Johann Sebastian Bach). Perhaps this is the issue for all music in worship. Perhaps we have lowered our expectations of music's role in worship and have given over our responsibility to the contemporary gods of popularity and success, more concerned about whether our choices will be liked, rather than whether or not they will be right. Perhaps we need to reclaim wholeheartedly a belief that indeed sound in worship is the shaping force we have sometimes claimed it to be. And maybe the music of the church of the next generation will be an eclectic mixture of old and new, familiar and foreign, experimental and safe, the much-loved and that which waits to be loved. *Soli Deo gloria!*

Chapter 11

Church Music as Icon: Vehicle of Worship or Idol

by Dietrich Bartel

In the past year, I have joined the ranks of Windows 95 users. When I start up my computer (it is colorfully called "booting" the computer, suggesting a much more violent activity than it in fact is) I am greeted by a screen exhibiting numerous colorful and imaginative little pictures or "icons" (the Greek word for "image, likeness"), which, when clicked on with the mouse, transport me into a myriad of cyberspace worlds. Not only can it take me to a drafting table, a composer's desk, or an accounting journal, but I can also launch myself into worlds unknown, traveling at will by the click of my mouse. And yet, negotiating this world of bits and bytes can also lead to distraction! How many of us have not experienced the frustration of our computers freezing up! For the uninitiated, this has nothing to do with Winnipeg winters! It is simply that things don't work any more. Everything comes to a standstill. You can click till the cows come home, but nothing happens. It is as if the icons have died. There they sit, still looking quite pretty on our fancy color monitors, but they remain quite useless. Where just a minute ago they were the gateway to new screens, new menus, new web sites, they are now quite impotent little pictures. They have become dead icons.

Have you ever wondered who thought of calling these little computer images "icons," that venerable term which signifies portrayals of holy personages in the world of Eastern Orthodoxy? Certainly we must agree that the analogy, accidental as it might be, is an intriguing one. There it is, that little picture on your computer screen, whose only purpose is to lead you to other menus, other programs, other worlds; a stylized image, quite useless on its own with just enough of a message to let you know where it might take you. Each one of those pictures is like a little doorway, a link to another reality. Surely it must have been a good Orthodox believer who thought to name these things "icons."

The icon and Eastern Orthodoxy

To avoid straining this icon-analogy, let us now consider Eastern Orthodoxy and the icon. For here too the icon is a doorway to another reality, a link between the human and the divine, a window into the kingdom of God and a bond with all those who have gone before us. Eastern Christian Orthodoxy has not suffered from the secular materialism that has marked Western Christianity since the Renaissance. In Eastern Orthodoxy, the icon fully retains both its symbolic form and its transcendent nature. When Orthodox worshipers venerate an icon, they are not worshiping an image but rather are acknowledging the grace of God at work in this world in the lives of believers—the saints and the martyrs who have gone before us—transforming humans into the likeness of God by the power of the Holy Spirit (Eph. 4:24). For example, in venerating an icon of Mary, the "Mother of God," the Orthodox worshiper is acknowledging that God chose the "servant of the Lord" (Luke 1:38) to work out the divine act of salvation, that this servant of the almighty Creator willingly submitted to God's call, and that we, like Mary, are called to carry Christ into the world. In venerating an icon of a saint or martyr, the worshiper is acknowledging that God is at work in the lives of followers of Christ, that through the grace of God and the power of the Holy Spirit, God transforms believers into God's own likeness. We are to "put away your former way of life, your old self, corrupt and deluded by its lusts, and to be renewed in the spirit of your minds, and to clothe yourselves with the new self, created according to the likeness [icon] of God in true righteousness and holiness" (Eph. 4:22-24). In fact, the icon is understood more as theology in color rather than the Bible in pictures.

The Orthodox justification for the use of icons is indeed a convincing one: in Jesus Christ, God is revealed to humanity in a material form. In this sense, God has become the first and the greatest iconographer. Jesus is not a second or a rival God, but God incarnate, the Word made flesh. To see Jesus is to see God (John 14:9). Jesus himself has become the icon of God (Col. 1:15), not pointing to human flesh and bones but to the work of the eternal Creator. To portray Jesus in an icon is not merely to paint a human figure but to represent the truest and greatest icon of God.

However, Jesus Christ as God incarnate is not the only icon of God. We too, created in God's image, are icons. Each one of us is therefore also a living icon of God. Therefore, our goal in life is *theosis*: to become better icons of God, more closely reflecting the divine image in our lives. Our purpose is to proceed from the image of God to the likeness of God. While we have been created in the image of God, only by the grace of God and the power of the Holy Spirit can we be transformed into the likeness of Jesus Christ, the ultimate and perfect icon of God. In understanding ourselves as icons of the divine Creator, we must view each other, our neighbors, and fellow human beings in a similar light. We are surrounded by icons of God in our daily life and work. This view takes all the abstraction out of Jesus' statement, "Truly I tell you, just as you did it to one of the least of these who are members of my family, you did it to me" (Matt. 25:40). In his discussion of icons, Anthony

Coniaris provides the following illustration:

> *A Sunday school teacher once said to her first-grade*
> *class, "You know how you feel when you draw a pic-*
> *ture. You want everybody to see it and admire it*
> *because you made it. That's how Jesus feels about you.*
> *You're the picture he draws. A little boy asked, "Is*
> ***everybody*** *Jesus' picture?" "That's right," said the*
> *teacher. "Even Annie?" "Yes." Suddenly a scrap of*
> *brown paper fluttered into the teacher's wastebasket.*
> *"I was going to put flypaper in Annie's milk," he said*
> *sadly, "only Jesus drew her, so I better not." That lit-*
> *tle boy captured a great truth. The most precious icon*
> *of God is man and woman. As we treat each living*
> *icon, so we treat God.*[1]

Our whole life, all our doing and being, is to be dedicated to this goal; it is to dictate how we view the world
and how we treat each other. Likewise, it is to determine
how we think about music and make music in our worship
together. But more about that later.

The icon is not like a photograph, merely depicting the
material world. And this is where Eastern Orthodox art differs so significantly from Western art since the Renaissance.
Eastern iconography does not wish to portray the subject
according to material reality but in a transcendent context,
just as Jesus was not just human but also God. (Orthodoxy
refers to Jesus as the God-Man, reflecting this duality.) The
icon is to depict the subjects, particularly the saints and
martyrs, as persons who have been transformed by the
Holy Spirit; that is, it is to portray the transcendent, not just
the material reality. Therefore, it must be symbolic, for realism ties the subject to the physical world, while abstraction
or stylization allows for a transcendent interpretation. The
icon opens a window to a different world, just like the icon
on the computer screen does. If it only points to its material self, it remains earthbound, a dead icon. It cannot call up
any further menus, take you to other programs, or visit

another web site.

The influence of Renaissance on visual art and music

The Eastern Orthodox view of the Renaissance mastery of the human form, of perspective, and of the realistic portrayal of light and shadow is far more negative than the Western art historian's view. In the art of Botticelli, da Vinci, Michelangelo, and all Western art since then, Orthodoxy sees a loss of the transcendent, with the human form and the material world replacing divine grace as both the subject and the object of art. As artistic representation becomes truer to the material world, it becomes less faithful to the transforming work of God's Holy Spirit; as it celebrates the world as we see it, it loses its power to evoke the world as it might be; as it turns toward human perception, it turns away from divine revelation. The Renaissance marks the beginning of realism in Western art: a mastery of perspective becomes desirable in painting; in sculpture, the realistic representation of the human form is regarded as an ideal; representations of Christ, of other biblical personages, and of saints and other religious or ecclesiastical subjects are now supposed to look more human, instead of representing the divine. In architecture, vertical and horizontal lines are given greater clarity, in order to please the human eye. And in music, an increasing emphasis is placed on text-interpretation, with the intention of making the music communicate with the audience. In music theory there is also a significant shift away from the mathematical disciplines toward the linguistic disciplines. This reflects a movement away from those disciplines that had traditionally been associated with theological speculation and toward those disciplines that focus on human communication, in other words, the humanities.

While all of this is not necessarily a negative development, it does lay the groundwork for the gradual erosion of the authority of the church and of religion. As we move

into the seventeenth century, we witness a growth of rationalism, leading eventually to the Cartesian credo: *cogito ero
sum,* I think, therefore I am. It is now human rationalism
that governs the determination of truth, replacing the
authority of religion and faith. The eighteenth century
increasingly views the arts and specifically music as a
medium to express personal sentiments, a development
that determines all the arts by the nineteenth century, the
era of Romanticism.

As Western thought becomes more human-centered,
art becomes more *self*-indulgent, "self" referring both to the
artist and the artwork. It is this phenomenon which Eastern
Christian thought finds unacceptable, leading some
Orthodox writers to proclaim Western representations of
Christ, the virgin Mary, the apostles, and the saints as being
depictions of the antichrist: human realism takes precedence over divine revelation; it becomes more important to
portray the humanness, the realism, the materialism or
worldliness of the subject than its symbolic content. The
birth of Western iconography (if there is such a thing) in the
early Renaissance marks the break between East and West.
Although the danger of this development was always recognized (as will be seen in Augustine's reflections on music
in the church), it is not until the Renaissance that the
change in emphasis begins to determine aesthetic and artistic principles. By the Baroque period, artistic composition is
judged by how well it moves the listener rather than on
how closely it adheres to the ecclesiastical tradition. By the
Enlightenment, the break is complete: an artwork is to
reflect the composer's mind instead of the mind of God.
For the first time, personal inspiration, imagination, and
novelty take precedence. There is talk of human creativity,
a concept that had until then remained solely in God's
domain. The human becomes the creator instead of God.
Art has become an idol instead of an icon. We still talk
about creativity today, rarely realizing that we are using
language that reflects the dethroning of God as the author

of all of creation, including music.

Just as visual artistic expression turns toward material-ism and realism in Western civilization since the Renaissance, so too musical expression is revolutionized with the birth of the modern era. Two significant develop-ments should be highlighted at this point. Just as in the visual arts, so too in the musical arts, the work of the indi-vidual artist as both its originator (creator) and its subject assumes much greater emphasis. Similarly, in music the focus of the composition becomes the human individual, both as subject and object of the artwork. Considering the first development, it is significant that, beginning with the dawn of the Renaissance in the fourteenth century, musical compositions are increasingly associated with a specific composer; composers, like painters and sculptors, sign their compositions. Throughout the following centuries, compositions are increasingly regarded as the reflections, interpretations, and products of the imagination of indi-viduals, rather than anonymous representations of the larger community. Increasingly, composers, like other artists, speak for themselves instead of their community. While this development is only marginally problematic at its outset, with the composers still firmly rooted in and accountable to their community, as time goes on it becomes a point of contention with the growing independence of composers and musicians. While Johann Sebastian Bach still understands himself as a servant of the church, the same cannot be said for Wolfgang Amadeus Mozart, who refuses to follow the wishes and demands of Archbishop Colloredo (as unreasonable as those demands may seem), deciding instead to go it on his own in Vienna.

By the nineteenth century, composers almost invariably speak for themselves, becoming their own compositions' subjects. Their guiding light is personal inspiration and experience rather than a collective *credo*; they become indi-vidual geniuses instead of accountable artisans of their community; their message becomes the Romantic lonely voice of the alienated artist instead of the articulation of a corporate vision. While the cantatas and passions of Bach are statements of faith reflecting the theology and beliefs of the Lutheran community, icons of the community out of which they arise and for whom they are written, the motets or the *German Requiem* of Johannes Brahms, for example, remain as individualized personal statements of belief. (An exception to this development might be found in the collection of motets of the late-nineteenth-century Catholic composer Anton Bruckner, a musician who clearly understands himself as a servant of the church and whose choral compositions reflect the influences of the Cecilian movement, an unabashedly church-music movement which, looking back to the musical practices of the sixteenth century, wished to counter the influences of secular music on the music of the church.)

A second development is that this shift of the musician from an accountable spokesperson to an individualistic creator would inevitably result in a monumental change in the way a composition was received by the listening audience. As the content or subject of musical composition shifted from being an articulation of a communally held vision or set of beliefs to individualistic self-expression, the music ceases to speak *for* the listener but rather speaks only *to* the listener, leaving the audience in a take-it-or-leave-it position. Like the musician, the listener also becomes self-indulgent. There is no longer any necessity to agree on the general validity of a composition: "After all, it is only the voice of one person, and there is nothing to say that I have to agree with that lone voice. My voice is just as valid as anyone else's. So you, sitting and listening next to me, don't have to agree with me either. For beauty is only "in the eye of the beholder"! With such a view of musical understanding and appreciation, a view to which the vast majority of Western twentieth-century ears (both inside and outside of the church) unwittingly subscribe, there is little chance of establishing a commonality of understanding regarding the content of a piece of music or its purpose and place in worship. And without this commonality, a musical composition is prevented from functioning as icon. When there is no agreement on the meaning of a symbol, its potential to symbolize has been annulled. That truth to which the symbol or icon, in this case the musical composition, points remains "in the eye of the beholder." The only thing left is the object of the symbol itself, which is now stripped of its power to point to anything beyond itself. It has become a dead icon or, indeed, an idol.

Music as icon

How then can music be regarded and function properly as an icon? I wish to focus on two aspects in particular. First, the music which we make, those sounds which we produce (either on stage or in worship), must become an icon to truly point to the Creator of heaven and earth. Second, the act of making music, the very ministry of music in our worship, must similarly point to our Creator in order to become transcendent.

At this point it might be helpful to suggest what happens when music becomes a dead icon, pointing only to itself and not beyond itself. I think we have all experienced instances and maybe have been involved in situations in which the focus has been on the music rather than on that to which it points. This is nothing new. Recall the words of Augustine in his *Confessions*:

> *When I call to mind the tears I shed at the songs of Thy Church, at the outset of my recovered faith, and how even now I am moved not by the singing but by what is sung, when they are sung with a clear and skillfully modulated voice, I then acknowledge the great utility of this custom. Yet when it happens to me to be more moved by the singing than by what is sung, I confess myself to have sinned criminally, and then I would rather not have heard the singing.*

Here Augustine makes the differentiation between being moved by the message of the music or by the music itself, in other words, by the music pointing beyond itself to another reality or pointing only to itself. Not only is the latter a dead icon, but in fact it has become an idol. And herein lies the dilemma of music in the church: is it functioning as an icon or as an idol?

Here in the West, Renaissance humanism, empirical materialism, and Enlightenment egocentricity or *self*-indulgence have unwittingly affected the way we think about music in the church. This is reflected, for example, in our discussion of styles instead of functions or purpose in our church music. The focus on style reflects a preoccupation with what music *is* instead of what it *does*. It reflects a concentration on the icon instead of on that to which the icon points. We would do well to be fully aware of this dilemma in our discussions of music in the church. What is it that informs us in our music ministry, in our discussions at music and worship committee meetings, in our choice of anthems and hymns, of preludes and postludes? Remember that if an icon is to function as such, nothing should impede its ability to point beyond itself. In the arena of church music, nothing should stand in its way to point beyond itself either, while at the same time, the music must possess sufficient clarity and content that it can, in fact, point toward a higher reality.

What, then, might some traits of such music be? What are some of the characteristics of music that functions as icon? First, worship music should be accessible. Just as the Orthodox worshiper has access to the icon, the worshiper needs to have access to the music to be able to touch it and be touched by it. In planning and choosing music for worship, consideration always needs to be given to the level of musical understanding of the particular body of worshipers. A number of years ago, while serving as music minister in a large congregation with a fine choir, I was able to include some rather challenging anthems and worship music in the Sunday morning services. Although the choir and I (as well as many in the congregation) were able to worship with and through the music, others were finding this more difficult. At this point the minister spoke a few words of wisdom which often come back to me: "Dietrich," he said, "you have to put the hay where not only the giraffes can get at it." He went on to explain that as a preacher, he continually had to remind himself not to preach toward the theology student or professor in the congregation, but toward those whose mother tongue was not Barth dogmatics. His call was not for poor quality "McAnthems" with little content, geared for the spiritual fast-food consumer, but rather for a somewhat less exotic menu which still included all the food groups and necessary nourishment. When we plan our worship music, we are giving shape to the icons through which the worshiper and God communicate with each other. This means that it must be accessible to the worshiper, while at the same time being sufficiently substantive to provide real and wholesome spiritual nourishment. It should be remembered that there is a great difference between simplicity and simplistic.

Not only should music of the church be accessible, but it also should seek to be inclusive in its accessibility. Our congregations are rarely very homogeneous. When ministering to a wide variety of people, it would hardly be appropriate to use music that excludes a significant number of worshipers. While it is impossible to serve everybody's needs all of the time, there should be enough variety in our church music to include as many worshipers as possible. When you walk into an Orthodox church, you don't find one icon for children, another one for youth, a different one for women, yet another for men, and so on. But neither do you find only one icon. Similarly, it would not be inappropriate to include folk, jazz, traditional, and gospel idioms as part of a given Sunday's music. But inclusivity in worship music implies more than simply avoiding narrowness in the choice of musical styles. It also implies the need for a wide range in the texts set to music, both in hymnody and in other worship music. Just as male and female were created in God's image, so too our worship music texts need to include male and female imagery; just as the Bible uses a great variety of imagery for God, so too our texts need to reflect this diversity of God-imagery; just as our congregations include a wide range of ethnic and cultural backgrounds, so too our music needs to speak these diverse languages. The narrower the musical menu of a congregation, the more limited is that congregation's music ministry in meeting the needs of diverse worshipers. Consequently, a narrow music ministry reflects and encourages a narrow congregation.

In recent times, Orthodox icons have become desirable art objects, bought and sold in antique shops and art galleries around the world. When these icons are removed from their liturgical contexts and end up on living room walls, they usually cease to function as icons. They become decorative wall hangings, works of art for art's sake instead of for worship's sake. The very same icon changes its function depending on its use or its location. Similarly, music even in worship, can become merely decorative, art for art's sake, entertainment instead of edification. When a piece of church music has no connection with the liturgy, when it is foreign to the context of the worship service, it hangs there like a picture on an art collector's living room wall. It might be too exclusive, or it might be liturgically inappropriate, like a Chopin waltz used as an offertory. It is not so much the style or genre of a piece of worship music which determines its potential to function as icon as its ability to communicate. Undoubtedly, there will be differences in the style of music from one congregation to the next, just like there are differences in musical literacy between individual worshipers. A Bach cantata or a jazz mass will make perfect sense in one congregation while it will need a lot of explanation in another. In such cases, a little musical interpretation can go a long way in making the icon come alive. I remember an instance where a Bach aria for soprano, oboe, and organ was to be incorporated into a worship service on a Sunday when the theme dealt with Jesus the Good Shepherd. We did the aria as part of the children's time, explaining to the children that the oboe represented Jesus as Shepherd, the voice represented a follower of Jesus (the vocal line followed the oboe in close imitation), while the bass line on the organ represented our footsteps. It worked, and not just for the children. Recently, I visited a congregation with a small college choir that had prepared mostly contemporary music, selections that had communicated very well to mixed or younger worshipers. This was a more elderly group of worshipers to whom the repertoire was foreign. In not taking the time to talk to the worshipers about the music, in not helping the icon come alive, worshipers found it difficult to worship through the music. The Bach aria would have needed very little explanation in this congregation, but a jazz setting of Psalm 46 did.

Icons are steeped in a long and venerable tradition. They connect the worshiper with past generations. They are a gift from one generation to the next. Similarly, music can connect us with past generations of worshipers. When we sing chants from a thousand years ago or gospel songs of the past century, we are united in worship with the thousands of believers who have gone before us. It is an awe-inspiring and reassuring thought to know that the music we touch, the hymns that touch us, are the same ones that have sounded in worship throughout the ages. Just stop for a moment and consider all those who in the past thousand years have sung "Veni Creator Spiritus," "Amazing Grace," or "Grosser Gott, wir loben dich." Who are we singing with when we lift our hearts and voices with those words and those melodies? Can we not hear all their voices echoing through the span of time? When I sing some of the bass lines of familiar hymns, it is as if I were transported back many years in time, standing next to my father as a young boy, his bass voice ringing in my ear. It is this connection which can give four-part singing in the Mennonite tradition such a powerful impact. However, not the specific style in and of itself, but its ability to invoke another reality, to open another window, lies at the heart of this icon.

Style and function in worship music

Over the past few decades, much energy has been devoted to the discussion regarding hymns and choruses in worship. As long as these discussions focus on stylistic questions (in true post-Enlightenment tradition), they are bound to remain unfruitful and divisive. As long as the brush strokes, the colors, the quality of the image of the icon remain in the foreground of the discussion, we are prevented from focusing on the real purpose of the icon. To make the icon come (or remain) alive, the focus must be on its function rather than on its aesthetic merit. Aesthetic questions regarding an icon only have value when they serve the greater question of the icon's ability to communicate, to transport the worshiper to another reality. If a musical composition, an anthem, a chorus, or a hymn does not fulfill its intended function because of the quality (or lack of quality), aesthetic questions may need to be addressed. For example, if the text of a piece of music is of questionable content, if the music detracts from the piece in question or adds nothing of significant value, if the presentation of the music distracts rather than contributes to worship, aesthetic or content questions (musical as well as textual) will need to be evaluated. In such a discussion, it is not enough to ascribe to the post-Enlightenment *credo*, "Beauty [truth] is in the eye of the beholder." For neither do we ascribe to this kind of thinking in our theology (e.g., If it feels good, it must be good). Some amount of expertise is required in making musical-aesthetic judgments, just as we require engineering expertise in building churches, the expertise of electricians in installing electrical wiring, etc. I would hardly feel safe in a building put up by someone who claims to not know anything about the craft but simply knows whatever he or she likes. This is much less a call for elitism than it is a criticism of post-Enlightenment thought. However, many people who are knowledgeable in the area of music, the trained musicians in our congregations, have been educated in institutions (such as university music schools) which place little or no emphasis on functional worship criteria in music, but rather, in the best tradition of post-Enlightenment aesthetics, value a composition solely on the basis of its aesthetic merit. Too often this thinking is brought into the arena of church music, without recognizing its fundamental conflict with the purpose and role of music in worship. It is not uncommon for some professionally trained musicians to choose music, be it an anthem or a hymn, not on the basis of how well it fits into worship or how appropriate it is for the occasion, but rather on the basis of the composition's musical merit. The finest composition will remain hanging on the wall as a lifeless icon, unless the worshipers are able to communicate with God through it.

Integrating the old and the new

Worship music in the church is characterized both by preservation of the past and by ongoing growth and change. Just as theological discussion continually finds new ways to articulate timeless truths, so too the music of the church continues to change in the light of new musical idioms and forms of expression. Four-part hymn singing is a wonderful legacy that many of us have inherited from past generations (although in the larger view of the history of church music, some congregations have begun to sing in four-part harmony relatively recently). It connects us with the past in a way that goes beyond explanation. However, in his book *Living Together*, Dietrich Bonhoeffer makes a most eloquent and convincing argument for unison hymn singing, quite understandable from his own tradition. We should always strive to "sing a new song to the Lord" but also be careful not to lose the enormous treasure and testament of faith that we have inherited from the past. We should also remember that our congregations increasingly represent a wide array of traditions, many of which do not share in a heritage of four-part singing. These rich and varied traditions are beautifully represented in *Hymnal: A Worship Book*. Through such a resource, we can grow to learn and appreciate a wider variety of icons, enabling us to embrace sisters and brothers of other traditions by worshiping our common Lord and Savior in new colors and forms.

Living icons

There is one more interpretation of icon that we should consider, namely, the individual as an icon of God, the human being as created in God's image. As Orthodoxy points out, we too are living icons, as Christ was the perfected icon of God. Through the work of God's Holy Spirit, we are being transformed from the image of God to the likeness of God, each one of us an icon of our Creator. That means that through us, through our lives, our actions, our words, God is to become visible. This is our great calling in life: to become clearer icons of God. Not only then is our music, but also our music making, to be an icon. The way we plan and choose our music, the way in which we discuss musical issues in worship, the way we sing and play in worship, all this is to be an icon of our Creator. When we sing together, we present a living image of God. This is a tremendous responsibility as well as an overwhelming gift. We, as God's living body, are collectively the icon of God to the world. We, as God's singing body, lifting our voices together with generations past and generations yet to come, are God's witnesses to the present and to the future. How will we paint this icon? How does the transcendent come to life in our music making? How do we allow the potter to mold this icon, to mold us and our music making?

There is no room here for divisiveness, for fractured icons. There is no room here for pride, for condescension, or for personal agendas.

A relatively new and wonderfully profound hymn with words by Fred Pratt Green has found its way into many new hymnals in the past few decades: "When in Our Music God Is Glorified." The text reads:

> *When in our music God is glorified,*
> *and adoration leaves no room for pride,*
> *it is as though the whole creation cried alleluia!*

The text can also be understood to imply that there might be times when God is not glorified in our music, when pride gets in the way of adoration, when fractures ruin the icon. It is then that the voice of creation crying alleluia is silenced. The icon has died. I wonder if the poet had ever considered adding a stanza that points in that direction:

> *But when our hymn begins itself to praise,*
> *when human voice the song of God betrays,*
> *how hollow then resounds the song we raise alleluia.*

The hymn continues with the second stanza dwelling further on the potential of music as a vehicle for worship:

> *How often, making music, we have found*
> *a new dimension in the world of sound,*
> *as worship moved us to a more profound alleluia!*

Here we have a picture of music as a living icon; through music we are brought to a new dimension; through sound we have been given a new vision, moving us to a more profound song of praise.

Summarizing then, let me propose that our music and our music making are living icons of God. The icon points to a new reality, linking us with the past and the future. The greatest and purest example of an icon is Jesus Christ, the Word made flesh. But it is a link that can be broken, a window that can be shattered. When the human object takes precedence over the divine subject, when material reality is celebrated over spiritual reality, the icon dies. Our music, too, can be understood as an icon, pointing beyond us and our efforts to a greater reality. This is possible when our music is marked by accessibility rather than obscurity, by simplicity rather than complexity, by inclusivity rather than exclusivity, by edification rather than entertainment. But above all, we realize that each one of us is an icon of God, created in God's image, and we are being transformed into God's likeness. When we yield to God's paintbrush, surely God is glorified, allowing all creation to cry: Alleluia!

ENDNOTE

1. Anthony M. Coniaris, *Introducing the Orthodox Church: Its Faith and Life* (Minneapolis: Light and Life Publishing Company), 177f.

Chapter 12

Silencing the Voice of the People: Effects of Changing Sanctuary Design

by J. Evan Kreider

From the time of its inception the Anabaptist movement has understood the importance of the voice of its laity.[1] Anabaptists were encouraged to own, study, and seek to understand the Bible for themselves. They learned to improvise rather than to rely on memorized or written prayers, and groups of laity sang new songs telling of their evangelical faith. As time passed, the voices of strong leaders increasingly predominated during the worship services, but the initial ideal of the laity having an important voice kept reemerging.

The worship experiences which have most profoundly affected my spiritual journey have been those in which I listened to the voice of the people as they beseeched God's mercy, collectively affirmed their living faith, and shared prayers or words of encouragement. The unparalleled joy I have experienced during the resounding outpouring of this voice in congregational singing has encouraged me to memorize more verses of songs than Scripture.

One of the primary reasons I continue to associate with the Anabaptist tradition is because of the ways my congregation has continued to give the laity a voice, whether during congregational singing, sharing time (when members share concerns or thoughts with the congregation), or times of free prayer (offered aloud from the pews by lay members). While sermons have certainly helped to form my thinking over the years, I find that I have been more profoundly influenced by what I have heard from the congregation; by God speaking to me through the voice of the people. In order for this voice to continue its important role within spiritual tradition, the gathered community of faith must ensure that we hear—in all its power—that which is said and sung by the community.

All of the components of worship services in Mennonite churches—the instrumental music, Scripture readings, sermons, prayers, drama, liturgical dance, or even the sharing of the peace—require that our congregations listen. Mennonites tend to forget, however, that congregational listening also occurs during participation in congregational singing and responsive readings. Anyone who performs music knows the importance of listening. Although we may not realize that we are in fact listening during the congregational singing, we immediately sense when we are in danger of going ahead or lagging behind, singing too loudly, or when we are singing the wrong verse. And our ears are constantly informing us about the overall effect of the congregation's singing or reading aloud in unison. Our congregational singing seems to make a far greater impression upon the minds of our little children than do all the sermons and children's stories combined. The participation of our young children in this singing assures them that they are accepted by their parents' community of faith and that they have the right to participate fully in its most public expression, that of adding their voices to the voice of the people. Given the importance of the "voice of the people" in the Anabaptist spiritual tradition, I would argue that the modern tendency to construct sanctuaries which are designed primarily for congregations to listen to the sounds produced from the stage (rather than to the sounds produced by the congregated laity) is profoundly altering, not only our congregational singing, but also our understanding of the importance of our relationship as individuals to our gathered community of faith.

This chapter calls attention to the unheralded role which the acoustical properties of our sanctuaries play in our worship services and urges that people give priority to discovering how the design and construction of our sanctuaries can assist rather than discourage congregational participation in communal acts of worship in the generations to come. The assumption underlying this argument is that the Anabaptist community must now find ways to ensure that the voice of its people continues to be heard. This principle offers an alternative view to theories of church growth and hierarchical church structures which assume that important statements come only from the stage.

The important role of music in our worship services

Visitors to some Mennonite congregations often comment on the emphasis music is given in our weekly worship services. I recently asked e-mail contributors to MennoLink to report on the amount of time their churches devoted to congregational singing and several other activities during the Sunday morning service (Table 1). The thirty-six respondents revealed that their worship services devoted a lot more time to congregational singing than to reading from the Bible, and some tended to spend nearly as much time in congregational singing as in listening to the sermon. For years, many of our churches have added an extended period of time for congregational singing (whether hymns or songs from overheads) before the worship service proper. The time spent singing prior to the service may surpass the time devoted to Scripture, prayer, and announcements combined. Though the musical repertoires of our congregations change, the importance of congregational singing itself remains a vital part of the Mennonite worship service. During this singing everybody is (whether consciously or not) listening to what everyone else is doing.[2]

Table 1
Times of Selected Activities in Sunday Morning Worship Services in 36 Mennonite/Mennonite Brethren Churches

Amount of time given in minutes, based on informal survey conducted through menn.rec.music@MennoLink.org and menno.voc.pastors@MennoLink.org during January and February 1997

	Worship Service	Hymns	Singing from Overheads	Bible Readings	Sermon
Maximum time	135	36	40	9	50
Minimum time	60	4	0	0	17
Average time	78	14	8	4	26

Changes in architectural design of Mennonite sanctuaries

Although Mennonites have generally borrowed musical repertoires from other denominations, the architectural designs of our sanctuaries have, for many years, remained resolutely utilitarian and were consequently visually distinct from those of the larger urban-based denominations. It was this very insistence on the construction of austere church buildings that unknowingly aided our congregational singing enormously, for the resonant acoustics of those plain rectangular wooden structures enhanced congregational singing in ways that are unimaginable to younger members now worshiping in modern sanctuaries.

With the economic prosperity of the 1960s, Mennonites started to move out of their isolated communities both physically and intellectually. For example, as the church growth movement swept through the churches in British Columbia in the 1980s, some developed an interest in imitating the architectural designs made popular by the fast-growing evangelical congregations. Slowly Mennonites abandoned their stance of architectural isolation. By the 1970s, many of our new sanctuaries could no longer be identified as buildings in which Mennonites worshiped, unless one first looked at the signboard perfectly positioned in the manicured lawn, beside the smooth hard-surfaced parking lot which was now worthy of holding our latest-model cars. The former ideal of living a simple lifestyle was dying both at home and at church.

It was in England's Winchester Cathedral that our two-year-old son first discovered the pleasure which resonant acoustics give anyone interested in vocalizing. The science of acoustical engineering is making remarkable progress these days, as certain internationally-renowned firms build upon complex mathematical formulae and develop increasingly sophisticated computer models.[3] Church building budgets, however, simply do not permit our committees to consult with any of these leading firms (such as ARTEC) in order to create the best acoustics possible, since their fees reflect the enormous amount of work and expertise required to ensure the best possible sound for the room's intended use.[4] But as we move from older architectural designs to newer ones, the changes in acoustics are certainly noticeable.

I recall hearing an enthusiastic Mennonite Brethren college choir of perhaps thirty voices sing in a recently constructed sanctuary in Clearbrook, British Columbia. Although I sensed that the musicians knew their music well, I observed that they were working hard to ensure that their singing could be heard in the acoustically deadened sanctuary and that they could hear each other within the choir. After the service, several concerned church members from the building committee asked why the sound of the congregational and choral singing was so poor in their new sanctuary. When I suggested what they must do to solve their problem, they like the rich young ruler turned sorrowfully away. Not long afterward, I heard a choir of perhaps twenty voices sing in that congregation's old sanctuary next door. I admired how effortlessly the amateur voices carried throughout the sanctuary, how the room's acoustics enhanced the singing of the small congregation, and how even a single voice could be heard reading Scripture or praying without any electronic amplification. A minister from the United States recently wrote to confirm that this experience is not unique to British Columbia's churches:

> *Our new building [built in the 1980s] has all the characteristics you mention: fan-shape, carpeting everywhere, padded benches. I've only been pastor here three years but have had numerous people tell me that the singing was so much better in the old building, which was wooden, rectangular, no carpeting, etc. Many young people no longer sing at all, and they certainly have never experienced the thrill of a vigorous gospel song ringing throughout the sanctuary. I am not a professional musician, but I have frequently noticed that I feel like I'm singing by myself ... And the grand piano sits partially behind a brick wall!*

How to deaden sanctuary acoustics and seriously hurt congregational singing

If the acoustics of two sanctuaries owned by the same congregation can differ so drastically, what causes the one to ring with our corporate singing and the other to act like a musical black hole? Stated simply, congregational singing is either enhanced or deadened by the room's shape and by the materials used in the construction of its floor, seating, walls, ceiling, and stage.[5]

The very shape of a sanctuary affects the sound, for

sound is reflected by the walls, floor, and ceiling. Over the centuries, the building of churches has demonstrated that longer rectangular sanctuaries reflect congregational singing more efficiently than do the more recent fan or even semicircular shapes. Concert halls have likewise shown that parallel walls enable sound to be distributed evenly throughout the entire room, though there are ways being developed for working with non-parallel structures. Since this utterly simple rectangular shape not only works superbly for congregational singing, but also for speaking, why are many of our congregations now opting for the fan-shaped sanctuary?

Part of the answer can be found in the recent concern about community and the visible symbolism of the community of faith gathered for corporate worship. Seeing the faces of other worshipers and not just the backs of their heads is now a priority. We are comforted by the sense of our being gathered together, as opposed to our being lined up in straight rows.[6] The exaggerated fan-shaped sanctuary can visually promote a heightened sense of community. This is noticeably increased as the room's fan-shape is opened toward the semicircle or beyond, as in the case of the College Mennonite Church in Goshen, Indiana. In my experience, however, the distribution of sound is never as successful in a fan-shaped sanctuary as in a rectangular one.[7]

My visits to our churches, however, suggest that the advantages or disadvantages presented by any particular room shape can be profoundly affected by certain building materials. Hard surfaces obviously reflect sound more readily than do softened surfaces such as those found in false ceilings or acoustical tile ("acoustical" implying a deadening rather than an enhancing of sound).

Of these building materials, one of the most significant is the presence or absence of wall-to-wall carpeting. I am tempted to entitle this section "Wall-to-wall church sanctuary carpeting: an invention of the devil," for even old

Screwtape himself could not have contrived a more efficient way to dampen our joy in worshiping God through congregational singing or sharing from the pews than have our determined Mennonite "carpeters." CARPETS ABSORB SOUND. Indeed, this is one of the main reasons we install carpeting in our homes, hotels, hospital lounges, airplanes, and waiting rooms. The argument usually posited is that we wish to create a dignified sanctuary, one promoting a quiet environment for our corporate worship. Some people do not want to hear our babies make any sound or our young children interrupt the lecture-hall atmosphere of the morning's sermon. And if soundproofing does not win the day for these people, finances do. The initial expenditure for wall-to-wall carpeting is often less than for equally beautiful wooden or tiled floors, and the cost of upkeep is thought to be less (until, of course, one realizes that carpeting has to be replaced about every twenty years at considerable expense!) Carpets are wonderful in high-traffic areas such as the aisles, but wall-to-wall carpets kill congregational singing; even hand clapping lacks vitality in a fully carpeted room. As far as the sanctuary's stage is concerned, I can think of no justifiable reason for it to be carpeted, especially if musicians are expected to use it and to project sound over it.

A Protestant church in the greater Vancouver area recently decided to replace its sanctuary's aging wall-to-wall carpet. Their astute organist asked whether the old carpet could possibly be removed and not be replaced for just one month so that the congregation could hear whether this made any difference for the sanctuary's acoustics. The congregation agreed to the experiment and before the designated trial period ended, they voted to sand and seal the wooden floor and leave all but the aisles uncarpeted, for the sounds of their piano, choir, and even their congregational singing were remarkably improved by the more resonant acoustics of their sanctuary. Choirs now beg to perform in this sanctuary. Contemporary praise songs have a ring to them, and amplified speaking is still heard with ease.

> *And all the people responded with a great shout when they praised the Lord, because the foundation of the house of the Lord was laid. But many of the priests and Levites and heads of families, old people who had seen the first house on its foundations, wept with a loud voice when they saw this house.* (Ezra 3:11b-12)

As I sit in the pews of one after another of our new (or newly remodeled) churches, the story told by Ezra comes to mind. In Ezra's day the older people wept when they realized how much less significant the new temple would be than the glorious one constructed by Solomon. Today older Mennonites lament the passing of the resonant acoustics of our older sanctuaries and with this the passing of enthusiastic congregational singing.

A significant part of this acoustical transformation is directly attributed to the change in pew design. The first change was that of adding padding to the seats of the pews. While padding the surfaces upon which we sit does not affect a room's acoustics when the congregation is seated in a full sanctuary, it does dampen congregational singing once the congregation rises to its feet, since the padding partly absorbs the singing of those people standing just above it one row back. Far greater problems arise, however, when our congregations wish to save money by purchasing pews or chairs that are covered with padding on the front and carpet on the back. Placing carpeting on the pew's back (the side supporting the hymnal rack) ensures that the voices of the people sitting behind each pew are largely absorbed by the surfaces of the pews in front of them. If you wish to kill congregational singing, purchase carpeted pews.

Changing dynamics within our worshiping communities of faith

Unfortunately, too many present-day Mennonite church designs seem to have been constructed without understanding that the shapes, the fully carpeted floors, and fully covered pews seriously hamper the ability of individuals to hear the total sound of the congregational singing. In sanctuaries suffering from dry acoustics, individuals sense that they are not being supported by others in their singing; they feel as though their individual voices are sticking out, and they consequently often respond by singing more quietly. This has a cumulative effect. For example, when my voice is not carrying very well in the acoustically dampened sanctuary, other people sense that I am not supporting them as they sing; everyone then tends to sing more quietly, regardless of the song's music, style, or text. In Vancouver's Willingdon Church, I have felt as though I was singing virtually by myself (or in an ensemble of those immediately surrounding me) even though over four hundred other people were singing at the same time. Only the amplified sounds of the worship team were capable of adequately filling this deadened space. Experiences such as these help me understand why, if I am surrounded by other enthusiastic singers in a resonant acoustical environment, I am far less self-conscious, and why I then tend to sing more joyfully, my spirit being filled with the assurance that I can unabashedly praise God through joining in congregational singing and responsive readings.

As musical styles and repertoires have undergone significant transformation during the past twenty years, so too has the style of those leading our congregational singing. In churches that sang without the help of musical instruments, our song leaders led by the sheer power of their voices. Although the leader's voice could be heard for the initial two measures, by the time the first musical phrase was completed, the leader's voice was submerged into the sound produced by the voices of the rest of the community of faith. What this said about Mennonites as a people was that we were equal before God within our community of faith. We, the congregation, heard ourselves worshiping our God collectively, as a community, through song. In this type of unaccompanied song leading at its best, the leader's voice is no longer heard as predominant but rather gives pride of place to the voice of the people.

One of the symbols of ecclesiastical power in the high liturgical traditions has been the bishop's staff, a visible sign of his special office, one that encourages people to listen carefully as he speaks. Today, for evangelicals worshiping in their increasingly deadened sanctuaries, one sign of authority is the microphone. Whosoever has access to the microphone can be heard and is therefore the person with the power at that particular moment. Those of us without microphones are relatively powerless.[8] The changes in our sanctuary acoustics have now created an acoustical gulf between those whose every whisper thunders to the farthest corner and those in the pews who would have to speak quite loudly indeed even to be noticed by those around them. Strangely, in some of the new churches, expensive microphones are required if a trained speaker is to be heard by even as few as seventy people.

With the advent of worship teams, congregations have installed impressive amplification systems that enable each musician to have a separate microphone.

> *[One] reason churches are building dead sanctuaries is because of a particular philosophy of church growth. If you want to be contemporary, the thought is you need high-tech sound systems for amplification. For a system to operate at its maximum (implying sound coming from the stage), you need a dead room. While this is great for events on the stage, it sounds the death knell for active congregational participation. The belief is that this kind of sanctuary (an ironic term, for I often want to flee from these places) coupled with the sound system, will provide the optimum arena for producing*

contemporary worship (meaning that of the worship team with drum, guitars, synthesizer, vocals)...

I believe there is an illusion occurring, whereby people believe that more volume coming from the front means a greater amount of participation occurs. In fact, it appears to be the opposite. We have lots of sound coming from the front, but many mouths are not moving. Two factors contribute to this: the sound from the front defeats any sound a participant can produce; and the songs are generally too high for men to sing.[9]

In some of the newer and truly deadened sanctuaries, two microphones are now required if the congregation is to hear the grand piano properly, an instrument which can otherwise be heard when playing with a full orchestra in a concert hall without any amplification whatsoever. As Tony Funk stated above, the increased amplification of worship teams essentially overpowers the congregation's efforts. This means that we are now on the verge of drowning out the voice of the people during congregational singing. Where will this lead? Will the time come when our churches will resort to giving each member in the pews a microphone so that congregational singing can once again ring out as in the days of old?

Suggestions

If a congregation is about to embark upon a remodeling or rebuilding campaign, why not have the congregation (not just its committee) collectively evaluate the designs used in other churches? To do this, I suggest that the congregation schedule worship services in various types of sanctuaries, old and new. During the visit, the speaking of the particular congregation's ministers could be listened to, the congregation's worship team and song leaders could lead in an extended period of singing songs with which the congregation is familiar, responsive readings could be read aloud, and sharing and prayers could be given from the pews. A wide range of architectural designs should be experienced by the congregation, and perhaps an architect, before expending money on something that might prove unsatisfactory to everybody.

Once the walls, floor, and ceiling of the new sanctuary have been built, the sanctuary should be tried out for sound just as was done when visiting other churches. The acoustics will be more lively than when all of the furniture is installed, but as construction continues, one can make changes in furnishings while it is still possible to do so. Some congregations have followed this procedure, bringing in rugs, blankets (imitating aisle carpets), and chairs from home (imitating pews) as they have sought to make final decisions about flooring and seating. Few Mennonites buy their cars without a test drive, but our approach to buying sanctuaries is often carried out more in good faith than with a careful weighing of the possibilities.

My heart goes out to people who are now in a church that has wall-to-wall carpets and sound-absorbing pews. I have friends who have either changed congregations so that they can once again enjoy singing in church or who have become resigned to the fact that their sanctuary's acoustics will not improve during their lifetime. To such people I can only say: Spread the word, invite people to your church, explain that you want them to hear how truly dead congregational singing can become, and then warn them not to follow your congregation's example. In order to rectify your acoustical problems, you may have to spend serious money.

I also suggest that churches select a design that promises to be more resonant rather than less. It is simple enough to add attractive banners, quilts, or a few rugs in order to absorb sound, but it is expensive to increase the sanctuary's resonance by replacing new pews or changing the floor covering.

When building a church and thinking about its costs, the question should be asked: How long does the congregation expect the new structure to serve them? Is this to be a one-generation church building, or one that will continue to be used for five hundred years? Invest accordingly; once the sanctuary is built, there is little most congregations can afford to do to change it significantly (to paraphrase Moses, the decisions of the parents will be visited upon their children and their children's children). People will be stuck with the building and its acoustical properties for years to come.

If we unthinkingly continue constructing sanctuaries whose acoustical properties discourage the voice of the people, we will quickly become denominations populated by spectators expecting to be entertained during worship; people whose main acts of participation will be those of listening and financial giving, instead of continuing to build upon our love of worshiping through congregational singing and sharing. God has been worshiped by the gathered community long before the beloved Psalms first resounded through the temple's resonant (uncarpeted) stone structure. Even the soft accompaniment of the harps of the temple's music teams was heard without amplification. I now look forward in faith to a possible revival of interest in improving the acoustics of our sanctuaries so that Mennonites can soon reclaim the voice of God's people.

ENDNOTES

1. It is indeed a pleasure to acknowledge the assistance I have received while writing this chapter. Several people read my draft and made invaluable suggestions: Alan Kreider (Regent's Park College, Oxford); Tony Funk (Columbia Bible College, Abbotsford, B.C.); James Fankhauser (School of Music, University of British Columbia); and Weldon Pries (Cambridge, Massachusetts). My study leave from the University of British Columbia was supported in part by a research grant graciously provided by the dean of the Arts Faculty.

2. For example, if you did not listen carefully while participating in congregational singing, how would you know when to start or stop, end each phrase, sing higher or lower (i.e., in the right key), or how to keep up with the beat. On the other hand, those of my friends who do not join in the congregational singing (usually having been told years ago in school or Sunday school that they should sing quietly or they would spoil the performance!) tell me that they listen carefully to the singing, following the texts closely. Some have suggested that they likely derive more benefit from the congregational singing than do those participating (for singers have to think about the notes and the performance, all while they are also worshiping). They have also been keen observers of recent acoustical changes.

3. Although software now exists to help people visualize how the proposed design for a sanctuary will look, I am not aware of any that enables us to hear what the singing of the congregation would sound like in a proposed sanctuary.

4. Many self-named "acoustical engineers" are in fact merely sound-system salesmen whose expertise is limited primarily to advising on how to deaden sanctuary acoustics and then amplify certain sounds electronically.

5. I wish to thank Weldon Pries, an architect in Cambridge, Massachusetts, for suggesting the six factors that might be considered: 1. the geometry of the volume; 2. the size of the volume (and audience); 3. the properties (materials) of the surfaces of the room itself and things within the room; 4. the articulation of the wall and ceiling surfaces (which break up the sounds and distribute them more evenly); 5. the height of the space; and

6. the sound reflective properties of the surfaces (how they thrust the sound toward the listeners).

6. Monasteries and medieval colleges often had relatively narrow rectangular sanctuaries. They divided their communities into two equal halves that sat facing each other—several rows along the north side facing the rows along the south side, each row being slightly higher than the one in front of it. Each monk or college student could see the faces of half of the gathered assembly. This formation, however, downplayed the primacy of the pulpit area, the area that is emphasized in evangelical sanctuary designs today.

7. Weldon Pries suggests that this problem can be addressed by adding undulating surfaces or irregular wall planes which provide a better distribution of sound throughout the room. Large flat walls and ceilings need to have their surfaces broken by irregular shapes. Old European opera houses featured extensive plaster decorations and ornamentations that we now realize were highly useful for reflecting the sound more evenly.

8. I once witnessed a church conference session in which someone speaking into the floor microphone was effectively silenced by the authorities who caused the floor microphones to cease working.

9. Private communication from Tony Funk, music professor at Columbia Bible College in Abbotsford, British Columbia.

Chapter 13

The Composer as Preacher [1]

by Leonard Jacob Enns

The church comes into existence through the preaching of the Word. [2]

Singing . . . was not ordained by God and must therefore be rooted out by the word and command of Christ. [3]

Teachings of Conrad Grebel

I have long been slightly uneasy about the fact that I teach music, direct a chapel choir, and compose music for worship, all at an institution bearing the name of Conrad Grebel. After two decades, however, I have grown accustomed to this provocative conundrum and have become increasingly convinced that, while "through the church the song goes on," [4] we could equally and perhaps as truthfully say, "through the song the church goes on." The composers of the song are also preaching the Word.

Assumptions

Music always speaks—either well or badly—whether as instrumental prelude, offertory, congregational hymn, choral response, or anthem. [5] Choices of music for worship and placement of music in worship require care and sensitivity and must always have as a guiding principle the needs of the particular worship service and the specific needs of worship at any given time in the service. The work of the composer will create an emotional context, establish a historical setting, and effect logical connections between *this* service and *that* hymn, whenever music is present and whether or not text is involved. A message of some sort is always communicated by the music, whether it is chosen wittingly or not. We do a disservice to our God, our worshiping community, and our own integrity as Christians bringing "heart and mind" in an offering of worship when we fail to acknowledge this powerful reality.

Furthermore, the sacral role of music is trivialized by unconsidered choices, and the integrity of the God-service (*Gottesdienst*) is compromised when worship is not the prime basis for our decisions. When Jane happens to show up just before the service, home from music school, and we add "special music" which has no liturgical function other than temporarily to suspend the flow of worship, our attention may in fact be drawn *away* from God-service. We admire her voice and are astonished at how beautifully she sings. However, worship may have been ruptured and displaced by a small concert.

Finally, I accept that music in worship carries various functions, some of them, admittedly, quite pedestrian. As it is likely that Pavlov's experiment would have been equally successful had he used a Mozart minuet, so Christian worship has embellished some of its necessary signal functions beyond the use of a bell or buzzer: now the service begins; when the third verse starts, children may leave for Sunday school, and so on.

Sermon versus music

The word (often the biblical narrative) has held a central position in Mennonite worship since the beginnings of Anabaptism. The presentation of the word has traditionally been seen as the task of the preacher, serving variously as proclamation, assurance, reconciliation, teaching, admonition, and so on.

Conrad Grebel would have wanted it just that way. Although his rule for worship—"no singing at the table"— was short-lived, it is sobering to be reminded of it. Grebel gives a long list of (unconvincing) reasons for banning music from worship.[6] However, Grebel's position serves as a useful starting point from which degrees of departure are imaginable to make room for the involvement of music in worship:

> - Normal speech inflections may give rise to reciting tones during the sermon, as informally stylized in some contemporary gospel-preaching traditions and formally stylized in the clerical chanting in some high church traditions.
> - The congregation may sing a text on a slow unison melody, with the music serving largely as a mechanical unifier.
> - Various types of more developed congregational singing are possible: from unison to singing in two or more parts; music with highly irregular and abstract (chant-like) durations, to physically engaging (dance-like) rhythms such as the Renaissance rhythms one finds in Luther's version of "Ein Feste Burg"[7]; from hymns to the singing of responses with explicitly liturgical functions.
> - Instruments, solo singers, and the choir might find a place alongside congregational singing, and various other art forms could be incorporated into worship.

In light of such a spectrum of possibilities and given the fact that there were virtually no purpose-built Anabaptist melodies, it is interesting to consider the very slow but highly ornamented style of singing preserved in some conservative Amish communities. In its own way, this style is akin to the medieval practice of "jubilation," in which the final syllable in an alleluia chant was drawn out in melodic ornamentation. Here, however, a similar process is applied to every syllable of the text. Is this a kind of subdued, slow-motion ecstasy? Perhaps. Yet, it is also instructive to consider this style a response to the original composer/preacher's voice, nuanced no doubt through the ravages of time and the effects of oral transmission. The original tunes, often bearing a Renaissance dance-like rhythm, are altered to such an extent that they are unrecognizable.[8] Thus the composer's voice, coming from outside the Anabaptist tradition, is silenced, since it is irrelevant to the purpose at hand. Consequently, only functions such as congregational coordination, immediate mnemonic purpose, and long-term historical archive remain. The process is akin to using a Renaissance painting to patch a hole in the kitchen wallpaper, and then painting the entire wall beige.

Today, however, half a millennium after Grebel, there is an increasingly strong interest in the intentional creation of various art forms for worship, and we find voices suggesting that the role of preaching might rightfully belong to more than the minister alone. Even the *Mennonite Encyclopedia*, in the entry on "Preaching" allows that, in Mennonite worship services, "other forms of 'sermon' are also utilized, such as readings, dialogue, drama, and use *of other arts as vehicle for proclamation.*" [9]

While Grebel removed music from worship (on specious grounds at best), the biblical voices in support of its use are well known and hardly need to be rehearsed here. Particular congregational practice will fall somewhere along the conceptual continuum between Grebel's austerity and the most ethereal and wordless utterings of the spirit, all functioning as acts of worship. For some Christians there is little connection between music and worship; for some, room may be made for "special music" with little thought given to its meaning in worship; for others music is integral to worship; and for others yet, worship is not conceivable outside of music. I find myself somewhere in the middle of this continuum and want to argue that, given the centrality of preaching in Mennonite worship, it is crucial that we acknowledge the impact of music and the important role that the composer has as preacher.

Preaching and composing

Preaching and composing have basic elements in common. There is little disagreement over the claim that good preaching requires an artistic guise, whether intentional or not; it has shape, flow, emotional drive, and other attributes popularly associated with music and the arts. Questions of style, beauty, and structure—more popularly associated with music, visual and performing arts—may rightly then be asked of preaching as well. And, although one would assume the normal point of departure for preaching to be one of intellectual discourse and rational communication, the entrée can just as effectively be made through the sensory, emotional side: witness the preaching of Martin Luther King. That is, preaching involves intellect and emotion. Good preaching will hold these in balance; manipulative, even abusive preaching will likely involve a gross imbalance toward the emotional side; downright boring preaching will involve an imbalance that, at its worst, would have no inflection or emotional communication whatsoever—the cardiac monitor showing a flat line.

Good music in worship has a similarly balanced appeal; it involves communication which engages both the intellect and the emotions in meaningful ways.[10] Although the entrée for music is popularly believed to be through the emotions and despite the assumption that musical compositions are some kind of received gift, pure "feeling in sound" if you will, all good music has logic, syntax, structure, and all of the normal attributes of a text-inspired sermon. Though the relative weight of perceived emotional and intellectual content is typically different between sermon and song, we must never let this dupe us into thinking that the first question to be asked of worship music is

an aesthetic one. In worship, primary questions will
involve the potential purpose of music and the choice of
music that is worthy of God-service, music that is an
"unblemished sacrifice."

In fact, as preaching may appeal strongly to the emotions at times, so music may, in some cases, appeal primarily to the intellect. An example from Bach illustrates this
point:

> *In his Cantata No. 77, "Du sollst Gott, deinen Herren,
> lieben," he sets Christ's commandment from Luke 10:27 in
> the opening chorus: 'You shall love the Lord your God with
> all your heart, and with all your soul, and with all your
> strength, and with all your mind; and your neighbor as
> yourself.' While the choir is singing this text, the trumpet
> plays the melody of a chorale which would have been famil-
> iar to Bach's congregation. The trumpet melody is from the
> chorale 'Dies sind die heil'gen zehn Gebot' (These are the
> ten holy commandments). Thus Christ's new command-
> ment is compositionally linked with those of the Old
> Testament, a linking which must be perceived intellectually
> to be appreciated.*[11]

As with preaching, music fails when it is characterized
by a gross imbalance between its intellectual and emotional elements, either becoming gushy and inappropriate, or
else exclusively cerebral and pointless as worship music.
Robert Shaw's words, although concerning music in general, can hardly be improved upon:

> *For finally, the understandings of the spirit are not easily
> come by. It takes a creative mind to receive the Creator's
> mind. It takes a holy spirit to receive the Holy Spirit. And
> 'just as I am' is not nearly good enough. There is no 'easy
> on,' 'easy off' for truth. There is no landscaped approach to
> beauty. You scratch and you scramble around intellectual
> granites, you try to defuse or tether your emotional
> tantrums, you pray for the day when your intellect and
> your instinct can coexist so that the brain need not calcify*

the heart nor the heart o'er flood and drown all reason.[12]

Thus the holding of intellect and emotion in graceful and expressive balance is a central characteristic of both sermon and music. This is not, however, to be confused with the concept of aesthetics in its strict sense. It is important to clarify that the issue of *aesthetics*, which commonly emerges in the same breath as *music*, is *not* the first consideration in worship music. Proper choice and placement within the liturgy, thorough preparation, and basic competence *are* factors; these are fundamental, and must be understood as given assumptions. Worship through music is a centuries-old activity. Aesthetics—the idea that music can exist purely for the experience it stimulates in the listener as a source of beauty or otherwise—is a relatively recent idea. It was not until the mid-eighteenth century that the idea emerged that a musical work could be valued for its aesthetic qualities (related to its structure, beauty, etc.) as distinct from its function in a specific social or religious context. In his book *Music Matters*, David Elliott defines the aesthetic experience as:

> *a special kind of emotional happening or disinterested pleasure that supposedly arises from a listener's exclusive concentration on the aesthetic qualities of a musical work, apart from any moral, social, religious, political, personal, or otherwise practical connection these qualities may embody, point to, or represent.*[13]

It is precisely the "moral, social, religious, political, personal, or otherwise practical connection" which is germane when we consider worship music. The question of aesthetics, of course, enters as a primary consideration when we deal with music in concert or educational situations. It is perhaps of some significance in dance music, popular music, and folk music. It is also worth considering in music for worship, but in this case, music is clearly a handmaid to another agenda and must always be chosen and prepared as such. A primary focus on aesthetics can lead to the abuse of the worship setting for the sake of music making.

Music as sermon

Music can function as sermon. When many voices are joined either in praise of the Creator or in acknowledgment of the human condition, then they are a metaphor for discipleship, community, and Christian calling. I want to claim that the very act of singing in worship constitutes an important lesson, and we would do well as members of the body of Christ to acknowledge its transformational power in our lives. I have been deeply saddened and frustrated by the way in which some modern electronically enhanced churches present an acoustically dead environment in which worshipers sit in plush comfort, but no longer hear each other singing as a body of believers. One wonders what the purpose of meeting as a group might be; the dead acoustics in such churches create a situation in which the worshiper no longer has any visceral/aural assurance of being part of a body and is forced into an experience in which the lesson must surely be that "my God and I" are all that matters—God speaks only through a disembodied loudspeaker, and my voice is the only other one I can hear. If buildings of this type continue to be built and people continue to worship in them, the theology of a priesthood of all believers will inevitably erode and be replaced by a theology involving some version of individualism at best.

In my worship experience, music (congregational singing in particular) has functioned as a tangible (aural/sensual) assurance that I am part of a *body* of believers; in its generic sense, congregational singing has functioned as an ever-present sermon about one understanding of the church, perhaps playing a role for the parishioner not dissimilar to that which stained glass windows played for the medieval peasants. Singing is a witness to a profound truth; it "preaches" a message simply by virtue of the fact that it is a participatory action, one in which various literal bodies are palpably *incorporated*, parable-like, into a symbol of the body of Christ.

Further, music "preaches," not only by virtue of its participatory requirements (at least in the case of congregational and choral singing), but also by virtue of the very medium which it is. A major shortcoming of Grebel's virtually exclusive emphasis on verbal expression in worship is the wholesale dismissal it represents of a large part of what constitutes the Christian believer. Surely we are more than talking heads, and the spiritual quest and concomitant issues of faith, ultimate concern, and ultimate commitment have equally to do with the numinous as with the rational.

Media guru Marshall McLuhan is helpful here. In distinguishing "hot" from "cool" media in *his* radical departure from the prevailing faith in the printed word, McLuhan helped us to see that supposedly precise media such as print (and I would include sermons) which he termed "hot" media, although full of information, barely address the whole sensory side of our humanity, while "cool" media such as television (and I would include music), though low on exact information content, address us at a broader sensory level. The medium, according to his argument, transforms our perception of the message.[14] I would argue that the medium of music in worship *is* itself a message; essentially, it is the message that God loves us as we are—human, with sinew and bone which can dance, with tear ducts that can cry, with hearts that can leap for joy, and lungs that can both sob and laugh. This message is not limited to the realm of music, but it is one which music can comfortably claim.

These are messages which music brings simply by virtue of its presence in our worship—that we are a community of believers and that our relationship with God involves our whole being. Therefore, it is important to recognize the fact that music is not something to be placed anywhere in a worship service simply because it happens to be a possibility. Music is often valued in some generic sense: Just as certain clothing is a good thing in worship, so is music. It adds color, a certain mood; it is functional, operating at times as a signal, sometimes as a time-filler. These are legitimate uses of music, and I have no argument with them, although we must always give care to the choices, even when music is used for a particular function. But our understanding of music in worship must go beyond that. It takes another intellectual step to accept the possibility that the *composer* might serve in a capacity parallel to that of the *preacher*, and that music also functions as *para-sermon*, and for that reason must be carefully considered in worship, since it has a very significant role there.

The warm underside to Grebel's hard dictum contra music is, in fact, a confirmation of the concept of composer as preacher. Harold S. Bender's simple statement of historical fact in his 1957 article on Mennonite church music actually lies at the heart of Grebel's position: "Since Mennonites have produced almost no composers of church music of their own . . . they have used the tunes of other Protestant churches."[15] Grebel would not have accepted this! In his day, the vast majority of available tunes (the musical sermons) were by Roman Catholic composers or they were secular tunes. It is no surprise that Conrad Grebel, knowing the sway which the composer holds over the listener or singer, came to his conclusion.[16] As a parallel to these musical options of the time, had Grebel had only existing sermons at his disposal and—presumably—only those written by Roman Catholic priests and had the ability of the "preacher" in early Anabaptist worship extended only to the point of reading the sermons of those Catholic priests as opposed to writing or improvising original sermons, then, surely, the nucleus of Mennonite worship might be something quite different from what it has become. Could it be that of all Anabaptists leaders, Grebel may have been the one who most fully understood the persuasive power of music and, given the existing options, chose his course out of recognition of that fact? His choice confirms that function of composer as preacher and is an encouragement to later generations to take that reality with the utmost seriousness whenever we are engaged in the most important act of the Christian community.

Composing as preaching

Despite the obvious circularity of the point, I want to claim that music has the ability to express realities for which words are inadequate, that music may provide virtually unmediated access to the spiritual dimension of our existence—the door to God, if you will. The spoken sermon is necessary, but the clarification, theological nuancing, and general particularity of words also creates a degree of mediation between the worshiper and God; music speaks (preaches) in a less mediated way and thus is also potentially more relevant to our spiritual dimension, thirst, and fulfillment. When appropriately written, chosen, and placed in worship, music is a path and often the most direct path to the Holy. In worship, music is at times a direct expression of the soul, speaking like the Spirit in "sighs too deep for words."[17] The work of the composer, then, is truly one of humble commitment, sensitivity, understanding, and seeking after truth. Little controversy would be generated by putting forth Bach as one of the greatest preacher-composers of the church. It is a testament to his deep spirituality and musical genius that his church music continues as staple fare even today. He was a preacher par excellence, writing a new sermon in cantata form for his Leipzig congregation for almost every Sunday for a three-year period in the 1720s and so fulfilling his commitment as cantor in a particular church at a particular time. Although his music and the whole canon of church music over the centuries is available and often relevant, it is still the case now as it was in Bach's day that new music must be written, and new musical sermons must be preached. Few preachers would rehearse the old sermons of the Reformation as normal worship fare, and, although works of music often have more to commend them and give them relevance over time than many sermons do, it is still the case that there is a need for new musical approaches and involvements in worship, to stand alongside more familiar traditional works.

The following lament over the present state of many churches could easily be transposed into a commentary on worship music that is drawn exclusively from the traditional canon:

> *Today, the churches resemble the valley of dry bones. People want spiritual bread and the breath of life as never before, but instead they are given meaningless rituals and limiting, enslaving dogmas. Sermons lack relevance, passion, and sustenance for mind or spirit. Scripture lessons tell us about distant people who knew the reality of God in their lives, but they are often impenetrable for us today because of their obscure references to places and tribes completely alien to our own experience. It all tends to remind one of a vast, archeological dig. On all sides, tradition takes precedence over compassion and honesty. An obsession with the past for its own sake prevents the church from facilitating a breakthrough of the divine Spirit to meet the needs of today.*[18]

This, translated into a comment on music, is too harsh a criticism. Nevertheless, it alerts us to the reality that could potentially result when worship music atrophies and never involves new compositions with contemporary perspectives on eternal questions. The church is a living reality, existing in time and changing with time, existing in space and changing from place to place. Composers live and work in the world of their contemporary church and speak in ways that are relevant to their particular church's experience; Bach would in all likelihood be amazed that his musical commentaries on the old Lutheran chorale tunes are still being used today, in a church with very different challenges and hungers than those which existed in his, with congregations for whom the chorale tunes (for instance) do not hold the same immediate meaning. I do not, for a moment, want to say that the old is irrelevant. It is still powerful in many cases. It still speaks and is relevant. But at the risk of over-generalizing, I would say that just as ministers help us grow up in our theological thinking, so composers bring us to a more vibrant and relevant experience of various spiritual dimensions—they help us grow up in our souls.

Two examples

This is not intended to be a technical analysis of how composers do their work, but a few general examples from recent worship music written for choirs may be helpful nevertheless. Arvo Pärt's *The Beatitudes* (1990) speaks to the church in a fresh way.[19] Christ's words are sung syllabically, in block chords, with no repetitions or other typical musical embellishments. Text phrases are separated from each other with large blocks of silence, thus allowing their meaning to sink in. Pärt uses a highly controlled musical language, treating the harmonies within each phrase in such a way that the effect is more one of shifting colors than of tension and release. Throughout the singing of *The Beatitudes*, however, there is a gentle yet implacable increase in musical intensity, taken over at its very peak by the wordless organ, which then restates all the preceding harmonies, in quick succession and in reverse order, finally returning to a gentle close, several octaves higher than the opening chord. Pärt preaches here through inversions: a silence follows each choral phrase—the inversion of sound; the organ ends the work—and the inversion of the choral beginning, both as a reversal of the harmonic order and as a textless statement. These inversions profoundly reinforce the basic upside-down quality that characterizes Christ's teaching: the poor shall inherit a kingdom; the hungry shall be filled; rejoice when you are reviled; and so on. Yet, we are left on a more elevated plane when the last organ sound dies out—both literally, in terms of the organ's pitch, and spiritually, in terms of a new vision of Christ's teaching. In these and many other ways, the work is a profound sermon.

Sometimes, the composer preaches in simpler ways. The overall gesture of a work may carry the main point of the sermon to another plane, just as a simple roof line may lead the eye up from the common table to the symbol of the cross or conversely, from the cross to the table, linking sacrifice and community in visual ways that go beyond the words we use to describe such a link. A similar effect is created in the short choral anthem "*O nata lux*," composed in 1980 by the late William Mathias.[20] Although I believe strongly that non-vernacular texts should always be translated for the congregation, either verbally or in print, this Latin anthem preaches even through the music alone. The first choral chord is a "thickened" C major triad, an octave above middle C (c',d',e',g'). The choral effect is one of ethereal height and elevation. Gradually, over the course of the anthem, the music descends to its final cadence—again an embellished C major chord but this time grounded two octaves below middle C (CC,GG,C,e,g,a,c). The effect of this final chord is one of warmth, peace, and comfort. The overall motion is one of bringing down, of incarnating the ethereal; it speaks simply as a gesture. The text, by Lawrence Housman, is a prayer to Jesus, the "Light of light" who "Didst deign in fleshly form to dwell" for assurance that final rest will be found: "Vouchsafe us when our race is run / In thy fair Body to be one." The music speaks of incarnation, grace, and assurance; it speaks directly, in an awe-filled and comforting voice.

Conclusion

Music is a way of knowing, and composing is a way of preaching. We are courting spiritual impoverishment when we depend only on words in worship, for just as verbal language leads inexorably to a richer intellectual life and potentially to a more nuanced theology as the language itself develops, so music feeds and enriches the spiritual life. It can speak to and for the soul in increasingly meaningful ways as our experience and exposure to its language develops. At the end of her poem, *Song of Enough,* Julia Kasdorf expresses what for many is a sensitive issue:

> When he came home
> from college, dreaming at last in English,
> he reached for words that didn't exist
> in Pennsylvania Dutch to talk with his aunts,
> and for the first time wondered what you could think
> if all you spoke was a language with words enough
> for cooking and farm work and gossip.[21]

The soul often reaches for words that don't exist in spoken language. Those nonexistent words are the natural language of music, and music is a natural language for worship—the "English" of the soul.

In his foreword to Westermeyer's *The Church Musician,* Martin Marty claims that the fundamental activity of the people of God is worship and liturgy, and that "they come to unity in praise by praying together and by singing together—lead by the *cantor* who helps produce *the people's song.*"[22] Westermeyer goes on to ascribe the role of cantor to those who lead music in worship (variously the organist, song leader, choir, etc.); my argument has been that the more fundamental cantor, and the most influential one, is actually the composer. Later, Westermeyer quotes Karl Barth declaring of the Christian communion, "What we can and must say quite confidently is that the community which does not sing is not the community."[23] If a fundamental activity of the Christian community is singing—in its various dimensions as icon, communal activity, and sermon—then the composer has as much to do with the cohesion, identity, commitment, and spiritual life of the church as does the preacher.

The composer speaks *out of, for,* and *to* a particular age, society, and often congregation. The work of composing music for worship is a humbling and awe-filled task, and, apart from the necessary musical skills, the composer is charged with the same responsibilities as any other worship leader:

> *First, you need a sense of your own faith, or at least some idea of where you are in your pilgrimage. Second, you need to know what the people you serve believe. And third, you must be able to enter with empathy into their experience.*[24]

Although there is a place for a large diversity of appropriately chosen historical music in worship, a place and purpose also exists for the composer who preaches anew to the particular needs and realities of each era. When those who have ears truly hear, this sermon will enrich their worship, and—to twist the meaning of Grebel's instruction that singing be "rooted out"—it may in fact uproot a text-bound religiosity and give wings to the soul.

ENDNOTES

1. A modified version of this chapter was printed in *The Conrad Grebel Review* (Winter/Spring 1997). It appears here with permission.

2. Harold S. Bender, *Conrad Grebel: The Founder of the Swiss Brethren* (Goshen, Ind.: The Mennonite Historical Society, 1950), 204.

3. Ibid., 176.

4. From the late-fourth-century hymn *"Te Deum laudamus,"* translated in the nineteenth century as "Holy God, We Praise Thy Name" by Clarence Augustus Walworth. This is the opening hymn in *The Mennonite Hymnal* (Scottdale, Pa.: Herald Press, 1969).

5. I do not for a moment dispute the fact that the composer may speak as a quasi preacher in the concert hall and elsewhere (witness any performance of Britten's *War Requiem*, R. Murray Schafer's *Threnody*, and a host of others); our concern here, though, is music in the context of Christian worship.

6. "Grebel proves with nine numbered arguments that singing does not belong in worship:
   (1) there is no example or teaching about it in the New Testament;
   (2) it does not edify;
   (3) Paul forbids singing (Eph. 5, Col. 3); [*sic*!])
   (4) what the Scripture does not positively teach and command is forbidden;
   (5) Christ requires only the preaching of the Word;
   (6) human beings may not add to the Word;
   (7) singing is not justified as a means to eliminate the Mass;
   (8 and 9) it was not ordained of God and must therefore be rooted out by the word and command of Christ." See Bender, ibid., 176.

7. Although writing with a different purpose in mind and discussing a different repertoire entirely, I still find Mellers' characterization of the two rhythmic extremes, which he terms corporeal and spiritual, provocative: "as the term suggests, corporeal rhythm comes from bodily movement: from physical

gestures in time, associated with work or play. . . . spiritual
rhythm . . . tends to have no regular meter and no strong
accents. In effect it is liberative and, therefore, ecstasy-inducing.
. . . [It] can flourish only in a monadic music, and can survive
only with difficulty, if at all, in a music that is harmonically con-
ceived."
See Wilfrid Mellers, *Caliban Reborn: Renewal in Twentieth-Century
Music* (New York: Harper & Row Publishers, 1967), 3-4.

   8. For example, compare the music of "O Gott Vater" with
its assumed source tune, AUS TIEFER NOT. The original source
tune reflects a typical Renaissance dance-like rhythm:

♩ |♩♩♩ ♩ |♩♩♩ ♩ |♩♩♩ ♩♩|♩ ♩   The joyful nature of this
rhythm and any even remote
association with such a characteristic is entirely stamped out by
the quality of the melody in its current state and the manner of
singing employed—"to be sung very, very slowly."
See *Hymnal Worship Book,* and *Hymnal Accompaniment Handbook*
(Elgin, Ill.: Brethren Press; Newton, Kan.: Faith & Life Press;
Scottdale, Pa.: Mennonite Publishing House, 1993), 33 in both
sources.

   9. James H. Waltner, s.v. "Preaching," *The Mennonite
Encyclopedia*, vol. 5, (Scottdale, Pa.: Herald Press, 1990). My
emphases.

   10. See Leonard Enns, "Music: Intellect and Emotion," *The
Conrad Grebel Review* 2 (Spring 1984).

   11. Ibid., 94.

   12. Ibid., 105. Quoted there from *The Choral Journal* 23
(February 1983), 21.

   13. David J. Elliott, *Music Matters* (New York: Oxford
University Press, 1995), 23.

   14. Frank D. Zingrone, s.v. "McLuhan, Herbert Marshall,"
The Canadian Encyclopedia (Edmonton: Hurtig Publishers, 1988).

   15. Harold S. Bender, s.v. "Music, Church," *The Mennonite
Encyclopedia*, vol. 3, (Scottdale, Pa.: The Mennonite Publishing
House, 1957).

   16. "When Conrad Grebel objected even to singing in worship it should not be thought that he considered singing per se
as sin. After all, congregational singing as it developed in
Protestantism was unknown in 1524. He objected to singing
because the only singing known then was the chanting in the

Mass, and the Mass had become an abomination for them." From Walter Klassen, *Anabaptism: Neither Catholic nor Protestant* (Waterloo, Ont.: Conrad Press, 1981), 59.

17. Romans 8:26 (NRSV).

18. Tom Harpur, *Would You Believe?* (Toronto: McClelland and Stewart Inc., 1996), 230- 231.

19. Arvo Pärt, *The Beatitudes* for SATB choir and organ (Vienna: Universal Edition, 1990). Recorded by the Choir of King's College, Cambridge, on EMI Classics 72435 55096 28: Ikos.

20. William Mathias, "*O nata lux*" for unaccompanied choir, No. 3 from *Rex Gloriae* (London: Oxford University Press, 1982). Recorded by Christ Church Cathedral Choir on Nimbus Records NI 5243: William Mathias Church and Choral Music.

21. Julia Kasdorf, "Song of Enough" from *Sleeping Preacher* (Pittsburgh: University of Pittsburgh Press, 1991), 12.

22. Paul Westermeyer, *The Church Musician* (San Francisco: Harper & Row, 1988), x. (Marty's emphases)

23. Ibid., 32.

24. Ibid., 32.

Chapter 14

The Hymn Text Writer Facing the Twenty-First Century

by Jean Janzen

I am a writer writing about writing. As a poet who has written a few hymn texts, my comments will carry a certain bias and will tend toward my personal experience as a writer. I am, however, a poet who has all my life been in love with hymns. My mother's clear soprano voice, which could be heard over the entire congregation, vibrated around me before I was born. We sang hymns around the piano, all ten of us, and still do at family reunions.

The hymns of the church have shaped my faith in profound ways. My understanding of God and of the call to the kingdom of God is undergirded by the hymns I have sung and still sing. The power of carefully chosen words set to music is the chief form of art that we have known in the Mennonite church, and I am convinced of the great need for art in Christian worship. My own experience in our congregation (College Community, Mennonite Brethren, in Clovis, California) verifies its power—visual, literary, music, drama. Art awakens and probes, it supports truth, it exposes deceit, and it adds order and beauty to our corporate acts.

The main challenge for the hymn text writer, then, is to make art. Because the hymn is a crucial part of our worship and theology, the making of a new hymn requires our most excellent efforts. My hope is that the comments in this chapter will inspire, not only poets and writers, but also all who plan worship, as we look for ways to strengthen faith in worshipers in the coming century.

Hearing the silence

The first challenge for the writer facing the coming century is to disengage oneself from the noise of our times, to seek that place of silence in which we have room to experience a sense of awe and self-abandonment. This may sound rather odd and unrealistic in our busy lives, but I really believe that we enter our days and our worship too easily and blindly. Very little surprises us anymore; very little causes us to fall silent. From my experience with writing, unless I sit down with the blank page and without expectation, I will not be able to write a good poem. Some writers are hit by inspirational material as they walk and work, but the attitude of the heart at the beginning of any work of art is one of coming to that place beyond or before language and thought, to be in touch with the deep place within us from which the necessary image or thought arises.

This is the place where true worship begins—to be in awe of God and of one's own life and ability to think of God in a language. "Let all mortal flesh keep silence," the ancient hymn intones, "and with fear and trembling stand."[1] It is the attitude of kneeling, forehead to the floor, hands flat against the earth. It is the holiness to which Annie Dillard gives many names in her writings, the reason we really should wear crash helmets to church, if we mean what we say. We ask our holy God to be present with us, and who knows what could happen.[2]

When we begin a hymn text, we surround our expectations with the history of our lives, our church, our God, and this is history we must hear, as I will discuss in the next section. But first we abandon even that. We say that we don't know. The blank page lies before us as a symbol of our dependence on the Spirit to nudge upward and forward those sounds and thoughts that might possibly be our words in a poem or hymn. And then we know that our task is a gift and that what we may accomplish is at its source a gift.

But speak we must "or the stones would cry out."[3] And so the movement of the Word and our word continues in its holy dance. To the grand gesture of the Creator, we respond with our small gestures in words of gratitude and wonder, recognizing our weaknesses, inadequacy, and sinfulness, recognizing also the grace that is given. Our movement of faith and words rises toward the Holy One who is mysteriously present in the silence.

> *Open, Lord, my inward ear,*
> *and bid my heart rejoice!*
> *Bid my quiet spirit hear*
> *thy comfortable voice,*
> *never in the whirlwind found,*
> *or where earthquakes rock the place;*
> *still and silent is the sound,*
> *the whisper of thy grace.*[4]

Hearing our history

The second challenge for the hymn text writer in our complex and crowded time is to hear the history which has accumulated through the centuries and which enters the new century and the new millennium with each of us. This history is immense and profoundly important to our sense of where we are standing. It is the ancient story moving ever toward the final unfolding of God's intentions for his creation and creatures.

The history of the church is a foundational portion of that story. As Anabaptists we should know about the contributions of our story to the larger flow. This is not to deny the authenticity and contribution of any voice that rises out of that individual's understanding and experience, for that voice will echo its history and its social setting in some way. Yet our unique communal history is a treasure we may hold in a world where dissolution of communal belief has been a pattern for a century. Helen Vendler writes, "The radically uncertain philosophical stance of poets . . . has helped to give poetry the air of a constant experiment in thinking and feeling."[5] We no longer view art as historical record, aesthetic artifice, and vehicle for moral instruction; in our century we understand art as process, as experience. This stance frees art to become a more authentic, individualistic expression, and harmonizes with the "unknowing" of listening to silence. But it lacks a place from which to speak. Within the silence is the voice which waits and which calls us to see our story always intertwined with the story of God.

It is the challenge of the hymn text writer to hear that story in a time when we value most that which is new. To write a text that is fresh and memorable is our task. That we might be able to create that new text out of the stuff of our history is a possibility. Certainly it has been my experience. When a member of the *Hymnal* committee asked me to write some new texts, I could not imagine what I would write about; it had all been written by now, I thought. But when the committee sent me chunks of writing from four medieval mystics, asking if some of the images and phrases might prompt a new text, I was able to attempt it. In fact, the larger portion of my contribution of hymn texts has been based on these writings and the Psalms. The rich language of these mystics and their startling ways of speaking to God and about God gave me courage and a kind of mandate to set their thoughts and devotion into text settings for contemporary worship. Mechtild of Magdeburg speaks of the Spirit as "harpist" and the "strings of the harp as love."[6] Hildegard of Bingen names the Holy Spirit as "root of life" and "eternal vigor."[7] The sense of motion and vital activity of God in their lives lit the fires of my own imagination, and I found meters and language to create the texts.

The Psalms, our most ancient hymns, became the chief songs of the Reformation, and the only acceptable ones for some groups. They continue to be strong sources for hymnology, available to be chanted as they are written or to be reset to new meters and paraphrasing. My assignment to rewrite some archaic translations of Psalms set to Heinrich Schütz tunes for our hymnal gave me the opportunity to enter that rich tradition. The language, loaded with images and the plaintive and celebrant voice of the psalmist, set high standards for all hymn writers.

We are also challenged to hear the voices of our own Anabaptist writers and singers. In my visit to Holland last year, I was privileged to hear the professional early music group, Camerata Trajectina, perform a concert of the powerful songs of the martyrs and early believers, their testimonies, admonitions, and celebration. The compact disc recording offers an English translation of the Dutch, a first opportunity for us to read some of these songs in our own language. During this anniversary time of Menno Simon's birth, some contemporary composers have set some of his words to music. These sources could inspire more hymn texts in the future.

The Mennonites have been a singing people in times of persecution and in times of peace. Lester Hostetler wrote a half-century ago, "but we have produced no important hymnody of our own."[8] Even as we have placed great emphasis on the importance of congregational singing, our more than fifty hymnbooks published in America since the beginning of the nineteenth century show that we have mostly borrowed from others. While only a sprinkling of Anabaptist hymn writers appears in these collections, the new *Hymnal* includes more tunes and texts from our own community than any book before this, and the *Hymnal* committee continues to solicit new hymns for their ongoing publications to augment the *Hymnal*. The challenge, then, is to write what is new from the base of our history. This will include our response to contemporary issues, our concerns for peace and justice, as well as our continued calls to confession and faith.

> *I long for your commandments;*
> *your judgments all are good.*
> *Within your word is wisdom;*
> *your teaching understood*
> *are comfort to my spirit's need*
> *and in the night my solace.*
> *Your statutes are my song.*[9]

Hearing our bones, our souls

Most lasting pieces of literature have come from a place deep within the writer, what I call writing from the bone or the gut. The songs of the Bible, the prophecies, and the visions are supreme examples of words and concepts that come from deep within and communicate to others deeply. Through the centuries those poems and narratives which sustain and change humanity are those which still feel true to us when we read and sing them now. Listening to our bones and our souls means that we will be telling the truth about ourselves. It means that what matters most and what is often the hardest to express is what is indeed pushing us to try to find words for it. It means that we will write both the pain and the joy. It means that we will hear the searing words of our failings, our sins. It is where Jesus wants to make his home in us, where he asks us to stay, so that intimacy and holiness can meet. And it is from this place that our readers and singers will recognize what is true for them.

Listening to our bones also means that we are listening to our whole selves, body and spirit in unity. Biblical examples, again, support the references to the physical in order to understand spiritual concepts. The psalms are filled with images of nature and the body's dancing, groanings, and tears. Jesus uses metaphors of food, common household articles, and labor to demonstrate what the spiritual kingdom is about. The gift of incarnation is the highest example of what the united self can be. Writing hymn texts out of that kind of unity will allow language to emerge which can bring a wholeness to our understanding of God. When I read the words of Julian of Norwich as she refers to God as her mother who gave her birth and Christ as her mother who gives her food, I was astounded.[10] My own bodily experience as woman was verified, and I gained courage to set these words down into hymn form.

And deep within us we discover the strong need for beauty and order. In the rhythms of the seasons, of our bodies, of our days, and our work and play lies the pleasure of language and music. In the sounds we make with our lips and tongues is the possibility of an order that will give delight. The challenge to write beautiful hymn texts recognizes that the container for our swirling emotions, thoughts, and lives can give beauty and order. We have the opportunity to continue to find fresh language for historical expressions and for new understandings. We have the tools of education and example to help us create art. We have within us God's call and gift to offer our best efforts for language that is addressed to God in worship and petition.

When we write from our deep selves, we also find ourselves most in tune with others, even those of other cultures and expressions. This is the gift of making art, and in the church we know even more surely how it binds us together. Our new hymns will be ever more inclusive of gender, race, and age groups when we write the truth about ourselves.

And so we carry this treasure, our hymns, with us into the twenty-first century, this bearer of good news, of God's story, of our story. Next to the Bible, they are our best source for light and hope. We hold them tenderly and close, and we hold them out to others with our open hands and voices, for the story is not ours to possess. It is ours to give away. We can keep the art of our hymns alive if we will care for them and continue to write new ones that give honor to God by their truth and their excellence.

> *O blessed Love, your circling*
> *unites us, God and soul.*
> *From the beginning, your arms*
> *embrace and make us whole.*
> *Hold us in steps of mercy*
> *from which you never part,*
> *that we may know more fully*
> *the dances of your heart.*[11]

ENDNOTES

1. *Hymnal: A Worship Book* (Elgin, Ill.: Brethren Press; Newton, Kan.: Faith & Life Press; Scottdale, Pa.: Mennonite Publishing House), 463. Liturgy of St. James of Jerusalem, 5th C; tr. Gerard Moultrie, Lyra Eucharistica, 2nd ed., 1864.

2. Annie Dillard, *Teaching a Stone to Talk* (New York: Harper & Row, 1982), 40.

3. *The Bible, New Revised Standard Version*, Luke 19:40.

4. *Hymnal: A Worship Book*, 140. Charles Wesley.

5. Helen Vendler, ed., *Voices and Visions: The Poet in America* (New York: Random House, 1987), xxiv.

6. Mechtild of Magdeburg, tr. Lucy Menzies, *The Revelations of Mechtild of Magdeburg* (New York: Longmans, 1953), 51.

7. Hildegard of Bingen, Matthew Fox, ed., *Hildegard of Bingen's Book of Divine Works with Letters and Songs* (Santa Fe, N.M., 1987), 373 and 384.

8. Lester Hostetler, *Handbook to the Mennonite Hymnary* (Newton, Kan.: General Conference of Mennonite Churches of North America Board of Publications, 1949), xxix.

9. *Hymnal: A Worship Book*, 543. Jean Janzen, based on Psalm 119: 131-135.

10. Julian of Norwich, *Showings*, ed. Edmund College and James Walsh (New York: Paulist Press, 1978), 295-297.

11. *Hymnal: A Worship Book*, 45. Jean Janzen, based on the writings of Mechtild of Magdeburg.

About the Authors

Eleanor Kreider is a member of the Wood Green Mennonite Church in London, England. She lives in Oxford and currently teaches in the area of liturgy and worship at Regents Park College, Oxford. In addition to writing and speaking about worship, Eleanor actively serves as church musician, worship leader, and preacher. Her publications include *Enter His Gates: Fitting Worship Together* (Herald Press, 1990) and *Communion Shapes Character* (Herald Press, 1997).

John Rempel presently lives in New York, New York, and is minister of the Manhattan Mennonite Fellowship. John also serves as adjunct assistant professor at Seminary of the East, New York City. Prior to his current positions, he was the chaplain at Conrad Grebel College in Waterloo, Ontario. He is the author of *The Lord's Supper in Anabaptism* (Herald Press, 1993), as well as numerous articles and reviews.

Bernie Neufeld is a member of the Sargent Avenue Mennonite Church, Winnipeg, Manitoba, where he directed the church choir for twenty years and was employed as minister of music for ten years. Currently, he is on the faculty at Canadian Mennonite Bible College, Winnipeg. He teaches in the area of church music, theory, and conducting His choir tours and leadership in workshops have taken him to churches across Canada and into the United States. Bernie's work and his commitment to the church have been inspirational in the formation of this book.

Mary K. Oyer lives in Goshen, Indiana, and is a member of the College Mennonite Church. She has taught church music at Associated Mennonite Biblical Seminary, Elkhart, Indiana, and at Goshen College. Over this long span of teaching, she has been active in promoting the singing of hymns in congregations across the North American continent. Mary has provided major leadership in the formation of *The Mennonite Hymnal* (1969), *Exploring the Mennonite Hymnal: Handbook* (1983), *The Hymnal Sampler* (1989), and *Hymnal: A Worship Book* (1992). She has also authored numerous scholarly articles and essays.

Christine Longhurst is pastor of worship at River East Mennonite Brethren Church and an adjunct professor of church music and worship at Concord College in Winnipeg, Manitoba. Christine is active as a violinist and conductor and serves the community with seminars on the place of music in worship. She is also the editor of the hymnbook *Worship Together* (The Christian Press, 1995).

Gary Harder of Scarborough, Ontario, is pastor of the Toronto United Mennonite Church. He is a frequent speaker and writer on a variety of topics relating to theology, worship, and the nature of the church. Gary has formal training in music and has been active in providing leadership to music ministry in the church.

George D. Wiebe is a member of the Sargent Avenue Mennonite Church, Winnipeg, Manitoba, but has also served as minister of music at the North Kildonan Mennonite Church. He was on the music faculty at Canadian Mennonite Bible College in Winnipeg from 1954 to 1993. He continues to give church music workshops across the country on behalf of the college. George has taken a leadership role in the publication of three hymnals: *Gesangbuch der Mennoniten* (1965), *The Mennonite Hymnal* (1969), and *Hymnal: A Worship Book* (1992).

Marilyn Houser Hamm is a member of the Altona Mennonite Church in Altona, Manitoba, where she has served as minister of music. She was actively involved in the recent hymnal project which produced *Hymnal: A Worship Book* (1992) and has recorded *Hymnal Masterworks* (Faith & Life Press) for soul piano. Marilyn is a private instructor of piano and voice in the community. She composes and arranges music and resources congregations in the area of music in the church.

Jane-Ellen Grunau is a member of Langley Mennonite Fellowship, Langley, British Columbia. She serves on the congregation's committee that gives direction to the overall education of children in the church. Jane is employed part-time by the Abbotsford School Division as an elementary school teacher. She also directs a music school in her home.

Kenneth Nafziger is a member of the Park View Mennonite Church in Harrisonburg, Virginia, and professor of music at Eastern Mennonite University. Ken has served as the music editor of *Hymnal: A Worship Book* (1992) and as editor of *Accompaniment Handbook* (1993), a companion to this hymnal. A frequent resource person for seminars and workshops on music and worship, he is editor of *Hymnal Subscription Service* (Herald Press), which provides new music for the church.

Dietrich Bartel is a member of Bethel Mennonite Church in Winnipeg, Manitoba, and is an associate professor of music at Canadian Mennonite Bible College. He teaches in the areas of music history, organ, and children's music. Dietrich has been active in music ministry in non-Mennonite churches and in planning programs for community events like the Winnipeg Bach Festival.

J. Evan Kreider lives in Vancouver, British Columbia, and is a member in the Point Grey Fellowship. He is associate director of the School of Music at the University of British Columbia. He has provided leadership in the church through music ministry, worship leading, and administration. Evan has been published in numerous critical scholarly works and has written reviews and articles.

Leonard Jacob Enns attends Waterloo North Mennonite Church and is professor of music and chair of the department at Conrad Grebel College in Waterloo, Ontario. Leonard teaches in the areas of theory, composition, and choral music. As a composer, he has published over thirty compositions, including works for choirs, choirs and congregations, instrumental and vocal soloists, chamber ensembles, and full orchestras.

Jean Janzen is a member of College Community Mennonite Brethren Church in Clovis, California. She is a poet who teaches poetry writing at Fresno Pacific College, Eastern Mennonite University, and in Fresno public schools. Many of her poems and other writings have appeared in various publications. Jean's hymn texts are found in *Hymnal: A Worship Book* (1992) and *Worship Together* (1995), as well as in other denominational hymnals.